clearing
the clutter

clearing the clutter

for good feng shui

mary lambert

FRIEDMAN/FAIRFAX

PUBLISHERS

A Friedman/Fairfax Book
Please visit our website: www.metrobooks.com

This edition published by arrangement with Cima Books Ltd
First published in Great Britain in 2001 by Cima Books Ltd

Designer: Roger Daniels
Photo Researcher: Gabrielle Allen
Illustrators: Kate Simunek, Sam Wilson

Reproduced in Singapore by Alliance Graphics
Printed in Singapore by Tien Wah Press

5 7 9 10 8 6

Distributed by Sterling Publishing Company, Inc.
387 Park Avenue South
New York, NY 10016
Distributed in Canada by Sterling Publishing
Canadian Manda Group
One Atlantic Avenue, Suite 105
Toronto, Ontario, Canada M6K 3E7
Distributed in Australia by
Capricorn Link (Australia) Pty Ltd.
P.O Box 6651
Baulkham Hills Business Centre, NSW 2153, Australia

Contents

Introduction 6

You are your clutter! 8

Clearing out to move on 16

Clutter hotspots 28

The bedroom: where the spirit rests 32

The children's bedroom: peace and stimulation 38

The kitchen: a nurturing place 44

The hall: the "mouth" of the home 50

The living room: sociability and relaxation 54

The bathroom: purifying the soul 60

The office: creativity and prosperity 66

The attic: where memories live on 74

The car: clutter on the move 80

Purses & wallets: the walking clutter mountain 84

Energize with feng shui cures 86

Index 94

Acknowledgements 96

Introduction

An accumulation of clutter in our homes is something we all suffer from, but it is whether we manage to keep it under control, or whether it starts to control us, that is important. Feng shui is the ancient Chinese practice of furniture placement and energy flow in the home. Improving the flow of energy and creating good feng shui can bring about increased prosperity, better health, and increased personal success. To achieve good feng shui in the home, it is first essential to clear away clutter. This is a powerful process that cleanses the space, helping to bring about amazing changes in the occupants' lives. Other feng shui changes or cures can be implemented after the clear-out.

A major part of feng shui is controlling the flow of chi (energy) in the home. A feng shui consultant's aim, when she visits a client, is to manipulate and balance this energy, so that it moves positively through all the rooms. When chi enters the home and encounters obstructions, it slows down. Piles of clutter in a home create blockages that restrict the flow of chi, making it sluggish, and this has a detrimental effect on the inhabitants. The trouble is that clutter, once it starts to build up, attracts more of the same

and, before you know it, your home is a clutter nightmare. The sticky, slow energy that surrounds your junk makes you feel reluctant to progress in every area of your life, influencing you mentally, emotionally and spiritually.

MOVING ON

Clutter in this case refers to things that you no longer use or love (see pages 8, 16–17). The trouble with most of us is that we have a tendency to form a strong emotional attachment to our possessions. So, even when an object is no longer useful, we still keep it, convincing ourselves that one day we will use it again. It is the same with unwanted presents and strange things that we have inherited: we always associate the item with the person who gave it to us, and then we can't let it go. When we do finally manage to throw out or give such things away, the feeling is liberating. Hanging on to too many old possessions also keeps us linked to our past, and does not allow us to move on.

A NEW LIFE

The aim of *Clearing the Clutter for Good Feng Shui* is to help you begin the process of clearing out, because the longer you wait, the

harder it is to start. It explains why you are hoarding junk and how your life will change when you dispose of it, a little at a time. The major "clutter zones" in your home are identified, along with checklists and clutter-busting ideas. When your home is junk-free, there are plenty of ideas on boosting chi, while the final chapter shows you how to use feng shui enhancements like water features, plants, and crystals.

The possessions that you keep in the kitchen need to be thought about carefully as in every other area of the home.

By streamlining your home and removing things that are no longer needed, you will create a place that nurtures and embraces you. You will find out what you really want in life, and allow space for new people and exciting opportunities to enter your life.

You are Your Clutter!

Clutter clearing is a powerful process that will bring startling changes in your life. Don't add crystals and other feng shui enhancements until you have tackled your clutter, because they just will not work.

In cluttered areas of your home, chi (energy) stagnates, and once this stale energy has accumulated, it will grow even more. Junk mail, abandoned craft projects, newspapers waiting for recycling – all these constitute clutter. Clutter also means all those neglected items that you hide in corners, thinking you will make a decision about them later – but you never do. Avoiding a drastic clear-out can stem from a fear of the future, but once you commit to change, you will move on.

YOUR INNER SOUL

Your home is supposed to mirror your inner self, so mess and inactivity reflect something that is going on inside you. The chaos will also make you feel lethargic, stultified, and confused about what you want in your life. Once you have emptied your junk hoard, you will feel physically, emotionally, and spiritually liberated, and you will have opened the door to wonderful new opportunities.

What clearing out means

If your clutter is getting you down and you want to start getting rid of it, you are ready to make changes in your life to bring yourself closer to what you want. Don't underestimate the effects a clear-out can have on you. You may find it painful to get rid of possessions that you have kept for a long, long time, and feel that you cannot exist without them, even though an inner voice is telling you to let go. To do this, you need to evaluate honestly what is relevant to your life now and in the future.

Think positively: saying that you feel you will be happier when the clutter is gone is not enough. Make a list of short-term and long-term goals, such as changing careers, starting a new business, having more free time for artistic pursuits, creating an area for hobbies, or embarking on a new relationship. Setting goals makes de-junking easier, because you are mentally clearing the pathway to your dreams.

You will feel much happier when you have cleared out rooms such as the bedroom and installed a range of good storage units.

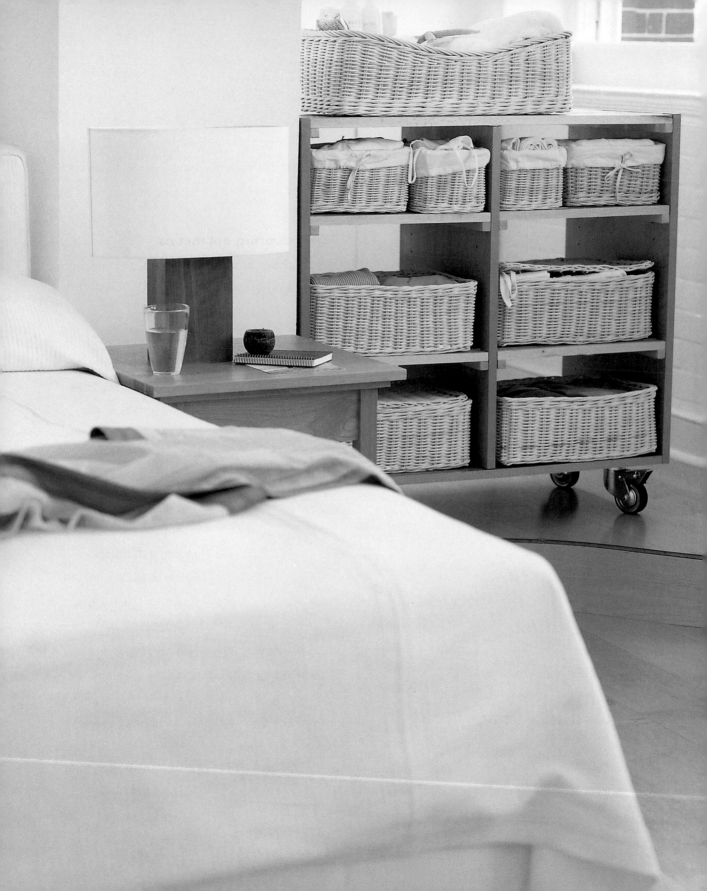

The flow of chi

According to the Chinese view of the universe, there is an invisible life force or energy, called chi, which flows through all things.

Manipulating and balancing the flow of chi in the home is a major part of feng shui practice. When chi moves freely, the atmosphere is bright, charged, and feels uplifting.

The chi that flows through the home needs to have a strong movement in order to have a positive and beneficial impact on all the people who live there. It enters through the front door and then meanders through the rooms in a spiraling movement (see right), finding an exit through a back door and windows.

Clutter is the biggest obstacle to a smooth flow of chi, because it creates a blockage that chi cannot easily get around. When this occurs in the porch and hall, for example, which are considered to be the "mouth" of the home, it prevents sufficient chi from entering. If there is mess everywhere, chi will struggle sluggishly around the house. This will in turn affect the occupants, making them feel confused or stuck in a rut. Feng shui consultants who are sensitive to energy flow may sense these stagnant areas by their stale, musty odor and a "sticky" feel.

Chi enters each room in the house and constantly forms spirals like wisps of smoke as it works its way from the door to the window. Chi also comes through the window and meanders towards the door.

THE ENERGY OF POSSESSIONS

When you surround yourself with articles that you love and often use, they emit a strong, vibrant energy that encourages the normal flow of chi and helps to produce an atmosphere that makes your life joyful and happy. Loved possessions seem to support and nurture you through invisible connecting strands. However, if you surround yourself with unwanted junk or useless, broken items, their negative emanations will only pull you down. The longer these piles of rubbish stay around, the worse their effects will be on you. Throw away everything that has no particular meaning for you, and you will shed a heaviness that will make you feel better mentally, physically, and spiritually.

When your home is a mess, it is difficult to find the things that you need. When your house keys are missing again, important letters have disappeared into the black hole that is a stack of junk mail, your cell phone has vanished and those shoes you so want to wear are buried somewhere at the back of the closet – it's time for action. This constant muddle mixes up the energy from these items, and you reflect this by becoming confused and stressed, rather than being calm and in command. So, by resolving your outer mess and kick-starting the flow of chi, your inner confusion will disappear and life will certainly start to improve.

If your home is full of junk, you will constantly have problems finding items that you regularly use such as your keys, cell phone, and favorite pair of shoes.

Tied to your past

One of the problems that we all have with clearing out clutter is that we form such a strong emotional attachment to some of our possessions. Gazing fondly at ornaments or other accessories that people have given us over the years makes us feel secure. We even hang on to mementos that are associated with an unhappy event, because we convince ourselves that we really do love them.

WHAT SHOULD YOU KEEP?

It is perfectly acceptable to keep some possessions that remind you of happy times, provided that when you look at them, you are filled with love. But if you have too many, your energies will be linked too strongly to your past, preventing new things from entering your life. Giving away or throwing out items that you strongly identify with can prove very painful emotionally, because it is like parting with a bit of yourself or rejecting a friend's generosity. When a friend selects a gift for you, it is chosen with a certain intention, often love, and these feelings then get tied up in the vibration of the object –

which is why we find it so hard to let go of it. However, the truth is that once you have relinquished some possessions, you often don't miss them at all. Also, if you give them to someone who will love them just as much as you did, you will feel good about it.

DO YOU NEED TO PRUNE YOUR POSSESSIONS?

◆ Do your possessions mainly reflect your past?

◆ Look at your home objectively and see what it reveals – do you sense fear of the future in the chaos you have created?

◆ If you gave away several objects from your living room, would it really have a negative effect on your life?

◆ Are your deep feelings about some of your possessions holding you back from a brighter, better future?

◆ Do you see dozens of memories in all your rooms, and realize no new ones are being created?

If you answer 'yes' to these questions, you definitely need to get rid of some stuff: so start pruning.

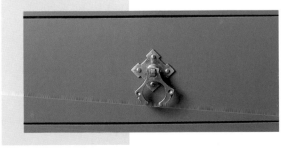

If you are finding it really hard to get rid of some items that you no longer use but which have wonderful memories, take photos of them and put them in bound books so when you throw them away you will not feel the loss so acutely.

RELEASING POSSESSIONS

It can be hard to give away or sell items inherited from deceased relatives. Even though you may never have liked an object, it relates to that person in the form of an emotional tie, or energy, that you are reluctant to sever.

You may believe that your possessions are visible symbols of the person you are. But when there are so many that they dominate your home, you may be subconsciously building a memorial to your past life – and if you do let something go, it seems as if part of you is going as well. But once you have started this process of release, you will not look back, and new energy will come flooding into your life.

Using the Pa Kua

If one area of your life is disastrous and nothing seems to improve it, check to see if clutter is the cause. The Pa Kua is a basic feng shui tool. It is an octagonal figure that corresponds to the cardinal points of the compass and what are called the four sub-directions. It contains eight ancient symbols, or trigrams, which are believed to be very powerful.

The Pa Kua has six rings. The first ring shows the trigrams; the second shows the Chinese name for the trigrams; the third ring relates to the five Chinese elements – Wood, Metal, and Earth, which have two directions, and Fire and Water, which have one. The fourth ring indicates the colors of each element, the fifth has the eight compass directions, and the sixth ring shows life aspirations. The southeast, for example, corresponds to wealth and prosperity, while the north is linked to career prospects. The Pa Kua can be placed on a plan of the whole house, or a single room, to make a feng shui diagnosis. Various parts of the home represent each life aspiration, and these can be activated to improve your luck in that area.

HOW CLUTTER AFFECTS YOUR LIFE

Now go around your home to see how your clutter affects your life aspirations. If your largest pile of mess is in your wealth section, this explains why your finances have been suffering. If some is in your marriage area, it can bring problems to an existing relationship or prevent a new one; in your recognition and fame section, you can become less popular and lack enthusiasm.

Recognition and Fame
South
Red
Fire
Li

Marriage and Romantic Happiness
Southwest
Yellow
Strong Earth
K'un

Wealth and Prosperity
Southeast
Green
Small Wood
Sun

Children
West
Metallic, White, Gold
Small Metal
Tui

Family and Health
East
Green, Brown
Strong Wood
Chen

Education and Knowledge
Northeast
Beige
Small Earth
Ken

Career Prospects
North
Black, Blue
Water
K'a

Mentors and Networking
Northwest
Metallic, White, Gold
Strong Metal
Chien

DRAWING A PLAN OF YOUR HOME

You need to find out where the eight life aspirations are in your home, so that you can see if they are being negatively affected by clutter.

◆ First, buy a good-quality orienteering compass. Then, with compass in hand, stand looking out of your front door to discover the direction that your home faces, making sure that you align the north end of the needle with the north point of the compass.

◆ Draw a scale plan of your home. Find the plan's center by drawing two diagonal lines from the corners and mark where they cross. Position the compass here.

◆ Mark the eight compass points on the plan: north, northeast, east, southeast, south, southwest, west, and northwest.

◆ Place a copy of the Pa Kua over the house plan, making sure that the compass points match the Pa Kua sections. Note which areas of your home relate to each life aspiration, and keep your notes for reference.

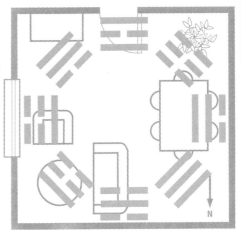

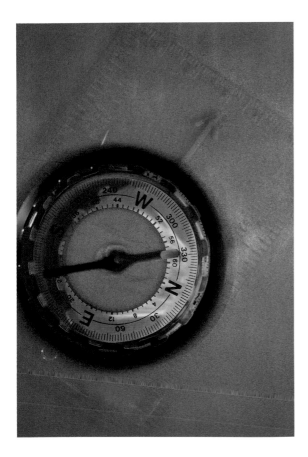

Clutter in your children's sector, for example, will inhibit your relationships with children and young people and hamper creativity; a blocked mentors and networking area shuts off support from friends and contacts, while a restricted career section will make your job seem like an endless struggle. Overflowing junk in your education sector limits your aptitude for learning and making good decisions. In your family area, clutter can cause regular conflict with family members.

Now that you know how the eight life aspiration areas of your home are afflicted, you can start by clearing out the worst area and see how fast changes happen.

An orienteering compass is all that you need to get the basic directions of your home.

Clearing Out to Move on

There is no doubt about it – a cluttered home brings about a cluttered mind. If your household is bursting with vast amounts of clutter, chi stagnates and will not flow smoothly through each room. This can have a negative effect on you – you may feel that your life is in a rut, your confidence may plummet, or you may suffer from depression or tiredness. Holding on to possessions that you are emotionally attached to can keep you linked to the past and will stop you from moving forward in life.

To find out if you are hoarding unnecessary junk, fill in the questionnaire opposite. Take no more than five minutes – your first answers are usually the most truthful. You can then start to work on the areas of your home that need the most attention.

Clearing out unwanted items from rooms such as the bathroom will help you to move on in your life.

ARE YOU A JUNK HOARDER?

This questionnaire will help you to assess just how much clutter has accumulated in your life. Score two points for a "Yes," one for a "Sometimes," and zero for a "No."

Yes   No   Sometimes

1 Your wardrobe is stuffed with clothes that you don't wear.

2 Odd socks and stockings that have seen better days lurk in bedroom drawers.

3 You keep magazines for more than a year.

4 You have several appliances that don't work, but you never get around to getting them fixed.

5 Piles of newspapers are stacked for recycling, but you never take them to the recycling center.

6 Old suntan lotion bottles and discarded make-up hibernate at the back of the bathroom cabinet.

7 You have old workout clothes and sports equipment, that have been used once and then relegated to the attic, never to be seen again.

8 You have a drawer full of mysterious old keys that don't seem to open anything.

9 Piles of old, often not very good, vacation photos of people that you don't remember are taking up space.

10 Your purse and wallet are awash with old notes, bus and train tickets, receipts from months ago, and other useless trivia.

11 Old files, papers, and pens that don't work have found a permanent home in your briefcase.

12 Your car is rattling with apple cores, cassette tapes that have died, and candy wrappers.

13 You are reluctant to invite friends to stay in your spare room because it has so much old furniture in it.

14 You have pieces of furniture that need repairing.

15 Unfashionable and unloved trinkets are tucked out of sight in one of your drawers.

16 Your garage is so full of junk that you can't get the car in it any more.

17 You have a collection of old, rusting garden equipment that you never use.

18 People keep tripping over all the boxes and other items that you store in the hall.

19 You still have theater or music concert programs from several years ago.

20 Your computer is crammed with files that you never refer to any more.

TOTAL SCORE

THE RESULTS

15–20
Your home and life are well and truly cluttered. It's time for drastic action, so figure out what you really want and what you can happily chuck out. Now consider what extra storage you need for the valued possessions that have survived the cull. Look at the storage you already have and decide how new furniture will fit in before rushing out and buying things.

10–14
Clutter is building up, so get a grip on it now.

5–9
You do not have a problem with clutter yet, but do monitor yourself.

Below 5
Your home is virtually clutter-free – so try to keep it that way.

Space-clearing rituals

De-junking each room (see pages 32–79) will help stagnant chi flow freely again. However, you may need a stronger method of changing the energy to suit different circumstances.

All the events that happen in a home create energies that become imprinted into its structure. Arguments and illness leave a stronger impression, and patterns that repeat themselves get deeply imprinted. So if, for example, the previous occupants of your home got divorced, there is a likelihood that the people before them did as well, and that this powerful residual energy (predecessor energy) will cause relationship problems for you.

To shift and cleanse lurking negative energies, so that your life is not affected detrimentally, you need to perform a space-clearing ritual.

ENERGY-BOOSTING TIPS

Use these tips as additional ways of improving your home's energy.

◆ Give your home a good spring-clean to lift the energy.

◆ Bring more energy in by opening all the doors and windows.

◆ Light candles to create yang, Fire energy.

◆ Arrange some fresh flowers, removing dried flowers or any dead or dying plants.

WHICH RITUAL DO I PERFORM?

There are some quite complicated rituals that require the services of an experienced space-clearing consultant, but you can do the following more simple techniques yourself.

Smudging: Using smoldering herbal smudge sticks are a popular way of cleansing the energy of a home (see page 22).

Aromatherapy oils: Add drops of essential oil to a mister filled with water, and spray the aromatic mist around your home to change the energy vibration (see page 24).

Clapping: This simple technique is used to shift energy that has become stuck in a room.

Incense: Trail the smoke from burning incense sticks around a room to change its energy levels (see page 26).

Natural salt: This traditional method of purification helps neutralize negative energies.

HOW TO BEGIN

Do not attempt space clearing if you are feeling physically or emotionally unwell, or if you are apprehensive about it for any reason. Avoid it also if you are menstruating, pregnant, or have an open cut. Clean your home well the day before, have a bath or shower before you start, and take off any jewelry you are wearing.

Candles can be used as basic energizers to lift the atmosphere in a specific room.

When to space-clear

If you just want to clear the energies in your home generally, try one of the space-clearing ceremonies detailed on the following pages. There are also particular times when creating an energy shift with these techniques will be beneficial to you and your family. Smudging and misting with essential oils are both very effective for deep cleansing. The other methods are best used in combination with these for intensive space clearing.

AFTER AN ARGUMENT

The oppressive atmosphere that lingers after a serious argument hangs like a black cloud. It can be very unsettling and, if it is not dispelled, it can adversely affect the mood of people who enter this room. Misting with essential oils of lavender, chamomile, or geranium works well. To remove emotional negativity, just mist with water on its own. Water creates negative ions that flood the atmosphere, creating an

Fresh-smelling herbs, such as sweetgrass, are used in dried form when smudging to space–clear. Other herbs, such as basil, lemon, and lavender, are used in essential oil form and are diluted with water in a mister. The solution is sprayed around the home or room to clear the atmosphere. Lavender essential oil has the same effect as neutral chi and is therefore particularly effective for clearing bad, stuck energy.

invigorating feeling, similar to the euphoria felt by the sea. Incense, too, can shift heaviness.

AFTER ILLNESS OR DEATH

Wash the bedlinens that were used in the sickroom, and do a space-clearing ceremony on the whole house so that you refresh all the energy. Thorough cleansing is advisable after death because, although it is a natural process, grief lingers, and sometimes the person's spirit does not move on easily. Smudging with

sweetgrass is powerful, and misting with essential oil of eucalyptus, lemon, tea tree, or rosemary lifts the atmosphere.

AFTER MOVING

History can repeat itself, so it is always a good idea to space-clear a new home, because there may be residual negative energies from previous owners. Smudging with sage or rosemary is beneficial, or you can mist with essential oil of lavender, sage, pine, fir, rosemary, or juniper. Use salt for extra cleansing power.

TO PROGRESS

Sometimes you feel at a dead end in your life, perhaps unable to make any positive progress. Or there may be a problem that you can't resolve. But by space-clearing your home, you can change the energy and allow solutions to enter. Clapping shifts trapped energy, while misting with basil, lemon, and clary sage can improve mental clarity. Smudging with cedar needles dispels a dull atmosphere.

Herb plants can help to energize a room, while herb aromas have been used by native cultures to literally "clear the air."

Space-clearing techniques

SMUDGING

In ancient times, smoke was used in religious ceremonies for purification, and to make a connection with the spirits of the air. Smudging is a Native American tradition, often used by well-known space-clearer Denise Linn. Bundles of tightly-bound, dried herbs are lit and allowed to smolder. The stick is then carefully carried around a chosen area so that its smoke will cleanse any negative energies and purify the atmosphere.

A number of different herbs can be used for smudging ceremonies, but the most popular ones are sage, sweetgrass, rosemary, and cedar needles. Sage was popular traditionally for its strong purification powers, while sweetgrass, with a distinctive, fresh smell similar to that of new-mown hay, was believed to effectively remove negative energies.

When you are smudging, make sure that you waft the smoke all round the room, including all the corners and nooks and crannies.

Buying herbs for smudging

Prepared herbal bundles for smudging, called smudge sticks, can be bought at natural health stores and some bookstores specializing in mind, body, and spirit titles. You can also make your own sticks by collecting herbs, tying the ends together with string, and hanging them upside-down in a cool place to dry.

The smudging ceremony

Light your smudge stick – you may need to blow on it to get it burning – and, when it is well lit, extinguish the flames, leaving the herbs smoldering. Always hold the stick over a fireproof dish in order to catch any sparks.

Before you begin to cleanse your home or a specific room, you should smudge yourself to clear your thoughts, emotions, and aura (your body's energy field). To do this, offer up your smoking herbs to the spirits then, opening out your hands, draw the smoke gently toward your eyes and then the rest of your face and head. Slowly carry on drawing the smoke to the rest of your body and your aura, asking for each area to be cleansed by it. This process will help to give you the energy to begin the purification of your home.

Smudging a room

Change into some casual or old clothes, wash your hands, and then, starting at the front door or the door of a specific room, walk clockwise around the room, holding the herbs and dish in one hand. With your free hand, waft the smoke along the walls and into all the corners, bookshelves, and closets. If the energy in one place feels heavier, waft the smoke into it more briskly. As you work, ask the spirit of the property to dispel negative energies and allow positive energy to flow there once more. Smudging

Sage and rosemary are two of the most popular herbs to use for space-clearing as they are good for removing negative energies.

reaches deeply embedded old energy and releases it. As you finish, close the door.

Repeat the process in other rooms, if necessary. When you have finished the ritual, extinguish the stick under running water, cut off the burned part and put away the stick (a small stick lasts for three smudging sessions, a large one for six or seven). Repeat the smudging technique every day, for two to three days, until the energy shifts, then smudge once a week as needed. Also, bear in mind that the smudging smoke is very pungent, so you will need to open windows and doors after each session to clear the atmosphere.

As you will have also cleansed your aura, your clothes and hair will smell of smoke, so you may need to wash your clothes and take a shower after the ceremony, and thoroughly wash your hair.

If you want to make your own smudge sticks, collect your chosen herbs, tie them with some string, and hang them upside down on a hook or nail to dry.

AROMATHERAPY

Essential oils are distilled naturally from herbs and plants. They have a wonderful smell and retain the life force, spirit, and energy of the plant from which they are extracted. They are normally extracted by steam distillation, which makes them around 70 per cent stronger than the plants or herbs from which they are derived.

We all react to smell, and different essential oils can soothe, relax, or uplift us. Some also have strong cleansing properties, which can help to clear negative energies from the home.

Lavender is a good oil for general cleansing. It is believed to be the equivalent of neutral chi so can really help to shift stubborn energy, such as predecessor energy, which is imprinted in a building by previous occupants.

Orange, lemongrass, lime, or peppermint oils are good for stimulating the atmosphere. For basic purification, the essential oils to use are juniper, sage, pine, or eucalyptus.

Finally, it is important that you like the aroma of the oils that you choose to mist with. It is always more effective and enjoyable to work with a scent that you really like.

Using the oils

Add a few drops of your chosen essential oil to a mister bottle filled with water and shake well. If you want to mist regularly, change the oil every couple of days, or keep the solution in a dark glass atomizer, as plastic can affect the oil's properties.

Stand still for a moment and close your eyes to set your intent for what you want the oils to achieve, and how you want the negative energies to be released. Then start at the door of the room to be cleansed and walk around it, spraying all around, paying particular attention to corners. Work your way through any other rooms that need cleansing. To bring about a dramatic change in energy, spray every day for a week, then once a week for maintenance. If you're using lavender oil to deal with difficult predecessor energy, it is a good idea to spray every room every day for 28 days, as this represents a complete cycle of chi.

To give yourself a quick boost, fill a small glass atomizer with water and one or two drops of your favorite essential oil. Mist around your head and body to revitalize your skin and to cleanse your aura.

CLAPPING

This is a very simple, but effective, technique for dispersing energy blockages and making shifts in your life. Think how clapping uplifts the atmosphere in a theater at the end of a performance.

Relax and set your intent for what you want to happen or change in your home. Stand with your feet slightly apart. Start in one corner: use small, quick claps to test the quality of the energy, and larger, louder claps to shift energy. The claps should sound crisp and clear if the energy is good; if they are muffled or dull, it normally means that the energy is poor. To get rid of this dead energy, clap up and down one corner, visualizing blocked energy there being dispersed as you do it. Move on around the room, making small claps, until you get to another corner that needs clearing. You can also "clap out" closets, and areas around electrical equipment to disperse the static electricity it generates.

Follow the same procedure in other rooms that need cleansing. When you have finished, rinse your hands under running water to remove any negative energy that may have clung to you. Repeat the clapping technique regularly so that you prevent any build-up of stale energy.

Clapping is a simple room cleansing technique, where you clap all around the room to lift stale energy.

INCENSE

If you walk into churches or temples in different parts of the world, you will often notice the pleasant, smoky aroma of incense burning. Incense sticks are easy to use and quickly raise the vibrational level of the energies in a room. There are different types of incense available; choose carefully because those made from synthetic substances may not have any effect on the energy in a room, and may even lower it. For powerful space-clearing, it is best to combine incense with another technique (see page 18).

The smell of incense also affects our senses. Hand-rolled varieties made from natural oils, gums, herbs, spices, and other ingredients all work well.

Using incense

If you are combining the use of incense with another space-clearing method such as misting with essential oils, just light an incense stick, place it in a holder, and leave it smoldering in the background.

If you are using incense by itself, close your eyes, concentrating hard, and focus on your intention to purify that particular room or your home in general. Put the incense in a holder to carry around. Light it, then blow it out so that it starts smoking and, starting at the door, slowly walk around the room wafting the smoke with your hand, concentrating on corners and dark areas. Repeat in other rooms, or set the incense on a side table and let it burn out. Make sure it is positioned safely. Never leave burning materials unattended.

SALT

For centuries, salt has been used by different cultures to cleanse and purify negative energies, because of its ability to absorb impurities from the air. Salt is particularly good for enhancing other space-clearing techniques (see page 18) rather than just being used on its own. Rock or sea salt, kept in a sealed container, is best.

Salt for space-clearing

Sprinkle lines of salt across every doorway, or place bowls of salt in corners and in the middle of rooms for deeper cleansing. Or, toss salt in the four corners of a room and anywhere that you sense that energy is stuck. Leave it for 24 hours, then remove it or sweep it up. If the energies in a room seem to have come to a complete standstill, renew the salt bowls daily for about a week.

MAKING A HOME ALTAR

When you have cleansed the energies in your home, you may want to create a special place to use for quiet contemplation or meditation for a short time each day. You can put a small altar or shrine here to help you focus your attention. Start by creating a focal point on the altar – this can be a representation of a religious icon or deity, like the Christian cross or the Buddah, a photograph of a natural place that inspires you, or a picture of someone or something who helps you spiritually. Include favorite crystals and fresh flowers, and burn a candle and your favorite incense to create a positive ambience whenever you use the altar. Set up the shrine in a spare room or corner, or, if you can't leave it out permanently, place all the elements on a tray and store it in a closet until needed.

Burning incense in a living room, for example, will bring in a wonderful aroma and dispel a bad atmosphere or any negativity after an argument.

Clutter Hotspots

The way your home looks reflects your personality. So, if it is disorganized and full of clutter, the way you run your life will be similar. If you have a family, you can't blame the disorder on them because they are also a reflection of you. Many of your rooms may be overloaded with junk (see pages 32–79), but there are also certain areas which, if allowed to become overcrowded with clutter, can symbolically restrict you from enjoying life.

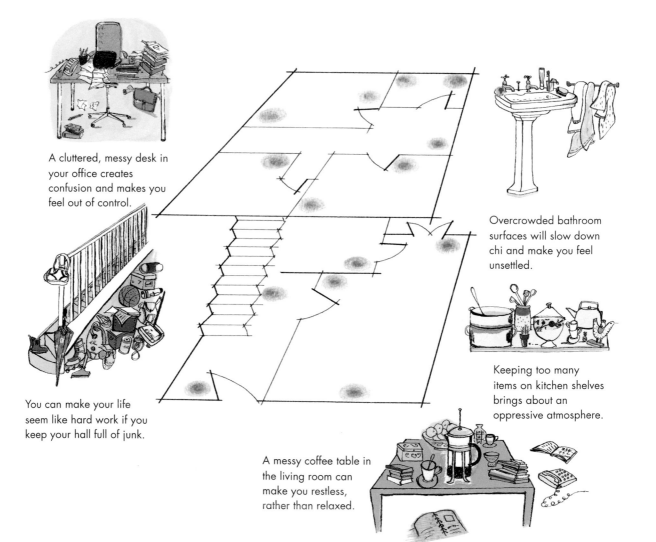

A cluttered, messy desk in your office creates confusion and makes you feel out of control.

You can make your life seem like hard work if you keep your hall full of junk.

Overcrowded bathroom surfaces will slow down chi and make you feel unsettled.

Keeping too many items on kitchen shelves brings about an oppressive atmosphere.

A messy coffee table in the living room can make you restless, rather than relaxed.

THE ENTRANCE AND HALL

This is considered to be the "mouth" of the home – where guests and friends enter and get their first impressions of where you live. It needs to be a bright, well-lit, welcoming environment that encourages chi to enter positively and meander through all the rooms in your home. All too often, this area is crowded with children's paraphernalia, shoes, bags, boxes, and newspapers, which make the energy slow and sluggish. If you have a pile of items that are stacked right by the entrance, it symbolizes life as being a real struggle, with new opportunities barred.

ATTICS

These are the places where we tend to store our past. These areas are therefore often full of mementos and memorabilia that simply restrain us so that we do not progress in life. After having a big clear-out, you will feel unburdened. Problems will no longer hang over you, and your aspirations for the future will no longer seem impossible.

BASEMENTS

Not everyone has a basement area, but if there is one in your house, it is likely to be jammed full of unwanted or unused junk. This area is believed to be linked to your subconscious mind. If it is brimming with paraphernalia, then there may be things in your past that you have not addressed, or problems that you have been meaning to resolve for some time. It is really important to keep your basement orderly, because if it is left neglected, it can have a detrimental effect on you, making you feel miserable, lethargic, and without direction in life. If you often feel weighed down by the troubles of the world, it could be that all the clutter lurking in the basement is the cause of this feeling of immobility.

THE BACK DOOR

This is where everything leaves your home and is, therefore, a symbolic organ of excretion. So if the area is full of junk, the analogy is that your home will become constipated, so it is important to keep it clear.

CORRIDORS AND PASSAGEWAYS

It is essential that chi flows easily through corridors to enable it to reach the upstairs or other parts of your home, so again any clutter will inhibit this process and should always be removed – common hotspots are either side of doorways and in wall recesses, so pay particular attention to these areas. If your corridors and passageways are overcrowded, these energy conduits of the home will create feelings of restriction and an inability to progress in life.

The declutter plan

Before you start work on the plan, first you need to assess what to keep or move, what to throw out, and what you need to give away. If you feel reluctant to do this, persevere, because clearing out rooms or spaces is therapeutic. It will release old energies and help to bring in fresh possibilities.

You may find that you have confused feelings about why you are so attached to certain objects that seem to have no further use in your life. Think about how you regard the space you live in – consciously and subconsciously – and how you can avoid letting your rooms or possessions take control of you in the future.

You do not have to throw everything out when you have your clear-out. In this bathroom, attractive storage baskets cleverly hold miscellaneous products.

ASSESSING YOUR JUNK

Now this is difficult. Go around your home with a pen and a writing pad and note down your main garbage areas, marking if they are large or small piles. Highlight the ones that irritate you the most, and start there first. Also pay attention to cluttered areas revealed by the Pa Kua (see page 14). If your career has been suffering and your career sector is full of trash, get rid of it and see how your working life improves. Start slowly, tackling one closet or a room at a time, or the task will be too overwhelming.

BAG IT

Get five heavy-duty garbage bags, or some strong cardboard boxes. Label the first bag "junk" (all unwanted articles to go to the dump), the second bag "thrift store or friends" (useful items you've grown bored with, but which other people might like, or which could be sold), the

It can be tempting to hide away unwanted goods in suitcases, but this just brings about stagnancy in this area.

third bag "things to be repaired or altered" (also include items for renovation) and the fourth bag "things to sort and move" (useful articles that need a home). Fill a fifth bag with transitional items you can't quite let go of yet (keep for six months: if you miss them, they can be reinstated, if not, get rid of them).

With clothes, be tough, and keep only those you enjoy wearing and put on regularly – probably only a small percentage. Try on the ones you're not sure about, and if they don't fit or you dislike them, get rid of them. Also, make a conscious decision never again to purchase anything that you're not absolutely happy with.

JUNK CHECKLIST

It's categorized as junk if:
◆ it's broken and cannot be fixed.
◆ you dislike it every time you look at it.
◆ it was an unwanted present.
◆ it's an outmoded style or doesn't fit.

It's not junk if:
◆ you look at it with love and good feelings.
◆ it's something you really enjoy using.
◆ your work is helped by it.

Where the Spirit Rests

A bedroom is a personal haven, a place for letting go of the worries of the day. Here we want to feel nurtured, and be able to regenerate our mind, emotions, and spirit. It is a sanctuary for sleeping, reading, dreaming, making love, and sharing any secrets or upsets. The room therefore should be calm and tranquil.

Wicker storage units blend in with the calm feeling of the bedroom. However, keep fresh flowers out of the room because they drain energy.

ENERGY GRIDLOCK

Chi moves into the messy bedroom and is held back from reaching the window by the crowded closet and chair full of clothes. Chi entering by window is slowed to the door by junk under the bed, the full dressing table and an overcrowded bookcase.

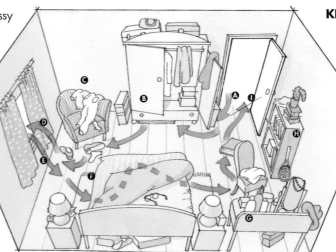

KEY: A chi enters; B overloaded closet; C overladen chair; D chi leaves; E chi comes in window; F clutter under bed; G overstacked dressing table; H full bookcase; I chi leaves.

ENERGY FREEWAY

Chi goes into the neat bedroom, traveling easily around the cleared closet and chair and out of the window. Chi comes in window and meanders through the empty under-bed space, over clear dressing table, and past the de-cluttered bookcase to leave the room.

KEY: A chi enters; B clutter removed from closet; C empty chair; D chi leaves; E chi comes in window; F no clutter under bed; G solid, supportive headboard; H soft lighting from rounded lamps; I natural wooden flooring; J ordered dressing table; K tidy bookcase with minimal books; L chi leaves.

The chi energy that flows through this area is very yin (passive) and will want to meander lazily. If your bedroom is crammed with too many items, the flow of chi will be hindered, denying you the relaxation and rejuvenation you seek. Clutter may also reveal the state of your love life. Is there a subconscious desire to keep a partner out of your life? Or does it reflect a chaotic marriage?

THE ENERGY TRAPS

Storing too much in the bedroom disturbs the harmonious flow of chi – so be firm with yourself.

Clothes: Are your closets and bureau drawers bulging with clothes? Most of us wear only 20 per cent of our clothes regularly. If you can't throw clothes away, you can stay too attached to the past. Piles of discarded clothes create stagnant energy, so hang up your clothes each night and avoid sleeping with a laundry hamper in the bedroom – yesterday's attire gives off dead energy.

Under the bed: It is tempting to store things under the bed, but if you do, they will create an energy blockage. Your bed should be a place that encourages good health and romantic happiness, but if there is heaviness underneath it, it can bring restless sleep and may also disrupt your love life.

On top of bureaus: Suitcases, bedding, and boxes towering on bureaus will feel oppressive and affect your sleep, sometimes causing you to wake with a headache. Their looming presence may cause sluggishness and a reluctance to get up.

The dressing table: De-junk cosmetics clutter. Discard those extreme lip and nail colors – you won't fall in love with them one day – along with virtually empty lotion and perfume bottles. Leave only fresh products that you use regularly.

A personal sanctuary

First, assess the room. Do you like its color and energy, and feel that it cossets you? Your bedroom needs to reflect your future dreams.

ROOM FOR RELATIONSHIPS?

If you want a partner, are you really allowing room for one to enter? If your room contains mementos from your last partner, you may also

A heaving closet full of many unworn clothes can keep you linked to your past. Dispense with what you don't need to make your "capsule closet" which can be neatly stored away, as above.

be subconsciously tying yourself to a past relationship. New lovers will absorb this energy and feel rejected by it. Also, a bed that you have shared with a long-term partner will still contain his or her energies, so either replace the bed or the mattress, or at least buy new bed linens. If you live with a partner, assess your space to see if the room reflects both of you; a troublesome relationship will normally be mirrored back at you. Remove, or at least cover at night, televisions, computers, and mirrored closet doors, as they are too yang. If you're happy on your own, appraise your room to see if it is a sensuous niche. Does its contents show where you are at, or where you want to be?

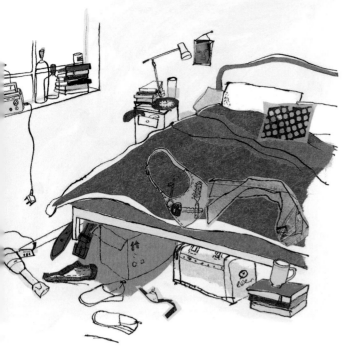

COLOR, MOOD, AND LIGHTING

The vibrational energy that comes from your bedroom colors has a profound affect on you. Good feng shui colors are shades of red – orange, soft pinks, and apricot shades promote sensuality. Pastel blues, greens, and lavender are calming and create a feeling of serenity.

Think carefully about lighting. Dimmer switches create a softer mood, while bedside lamps with rounded shades give a warm glow for night reading. Flickering candles add romance; incense, or the scent of geranium from an aromatherapy burner creates fragrant relaxation. Put out all candles before sleeping.

Junk that is thrown under the bed becomes stuck energy and can affect your health (top left). Clear out unnecessary goods and store your essentials in this blanket box (left). Place moveable items on top so that you can have easy access to its contents. Natural wood flooring encourages a good flow of chi.

Ordered bliss

Now you have appraised your bedroom possessions, you need to look at storage solutions to hide them all away and create the peaceful atmosphere that is so needed in this

By planning in adequate shelving units that will hold shirts, jumpers, T-shirts, tops, and other clothing, you can make your bedroom a serene and well-ordered environment.

room. Study the room and see if there are any alcoves where you could fit an extra unit. Remember you overall goal is clean, ordered surfaces and tidy chests and cabinets, so that the chi entering the bedroom flows smoothly.

STORAGE SOLUTIONS

Clothes and shoes Look at what you have left: is it really now a "capsule" closet of just your favorite items? Separate summer and

BEDROOM CLUTTER CHECKLIST

If your room is a clutter nightmare, search through everything, making your five distinct piles (see page 31).

◆ Clothes and shoes: Empty your closets and drawers, deciding what you really love to wear – and what you don't.

◆ Jewelry: Remove broken items and take out pieces hardly worn.

◆ Cosmetics, lotions, perfumes, and aftershaves: throw away any that are virtually finished.

◆ Bedding: If piled on top of the closet, store elsewhere; throw out old or torn linens.

◆ Books and magazines: Be ruthless and keep to a minimum. Too many books in the bedroom is not good feng shui.

◆ Boxes of old sports gear, broken appliances, and general clutter: If scattered around the room and under the bed, throw out now, or store properly elsewhere.

winter clothes, and store those that are not currently being used in a closet or in a suitcase in the spare room. If you have only one bedroom, see if you are making best use of the space available to you – tall, wicker or rattan-style units with several shelves come in different sizes and fit well in recessed corners. They can swallow up a stack of sweaters, tops, shirts, T-shirts, and shorts.

How about increasing your closet's efficiency by fitting tiered racks for your shoes, or maybe adding canvas or mesh hanging racks for sweaters and skirts? If your closet has shelves, slot in different-sized clear plastic boxes for view-at-a-glance storage. Multiple skirt and pants hangers also help maximize your hanging space.

Store socks, stockings, underwear, and ties in boxes that either fit neatly into drawers or partitioned boxes on shelves.

Linens and bedding Bulky duvets, pillows and bed linens can be hidden in blanket boxes or wicker baskets at the foot of the bed.

Cosmetics and jewelry Tidy current cosmetics into neat, clear plastic boxes with compartments that enable tubes or brushes to stand upright. A set of small, woven baskets would also work well. Sort jewelry into tiered boxes.

Books and magazines Keep only one or two current magazines here and minimal books. Place favorite books on a small bookshelf or in a bedside cabinet.

Miscellaneous items Don't store them in an under-bed drawer unit; keep elsewhere or in a stacking unit in the closet.

Handy plastic boxes can be slipped into narrow drawers to hold socks, underwear, or scarves.

Peace and Stimulation

Your children's bedroom is their own special place. As well as being somewhere to sleep, it is their refuge from the world, where they can play games, read, give rein to their creative abilities, settle down to homework, hang their favorite posters, entertain friends, and listen to the latest music.

Although primarily for rest, the room is also an area where children need stimulation for homework and hobbies, so it benefits from positive chi energy. If their bedroom is overcrowded with unloved toys, sports gear, or school items, the flow of chi will be hampered and this will make children unable to think clearly or to act in a positive way.

THE ENERGY TRAPS

Children are notoriously messy, often leaving toys and books strewn across the floor. But this trail of chaos disrupts the atmosphere and can disturb their sleep, so cajole them to tidy up on a regular basis.

Play or work areas If these are an explosion of cars, dolls, games, CDs, computer games, and schoolwork, it will distort chi and prevent good-quality sleep.

Overloaded closets If the doors will not shut because of all the goods stacked inside, a feeling of oppression will permeate the room (see page 20). Children may also subliminally worry that everything will fall out on top of

ENERGY GRIDLOCK

Chi moves into the children's messy bedroom and is stopped by an overladen closet. Its route to the window is further hampered by clothes and toys on the floor and clutter under the beds. Chi entering through the window is restricted on its way to the door by a crowded play table and books and clothes strewn on the floor.

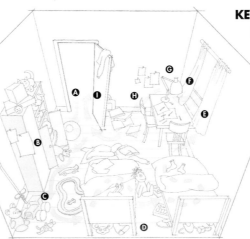

KEY: A chi enters; B bulging closet; C scattered clothes and toys; D clothes and toys under beds; E chi leaves; F chi flows in window; G jumbled play table; H books and toys piled on floor; I chi leaves.

Small hanging units add to the look of the bedroom and can display small painted toys.

ENERGY FREEWAY

Chi weaves into an ordered bedroom and flows evenly around a cleared closet and stored toys, and through empty under-bed space to the window. Chi proceeds through the window and slides over an ordered play table, and around the bare floor to the door.

KEY: A chi enters; B re-planned closet; C bag for dirty clothes; D toys stored in stacking boxes; E no mess under beds; F rounded bedside lamps; G fabric wallhanging to slow chi; H chi leaves; I chi comes in window; J structured play table; K desk lamp for schoolwork; L cleared floor; M chi leaves.

them – despite the fact that they created the situation in the first place.

Clothes Although children don't hang on to clothes because they are emotionally attached to them, they are adept at leaving them in scattered heaps, sources of stale energy that make the bedroom's atmosphere sluggish and dull.

Under the bed As with an adult's bedroom (see page 33), keep this area clear.

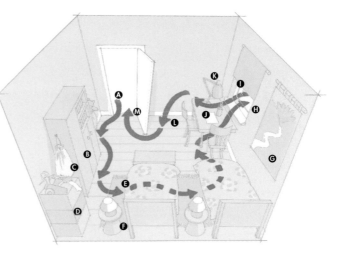

Keeping the children's bedroom tidy is a constant battle, so have plenty of tiered storage and make it a rule that all toys need to be put away at night.

A magical hideaway

Clearing up your children's bedroom will make you and them feel better – despite what they might say! But before you do this, pause briefly and study the room. Appraise the furniture, the paint color or wallpaper, the posters, and pictures. Do they reflect your children as they are today, or is the room still linked to the past? Have they been sleeping well, or possibly complaining of disturbed nights? Like an adult's bedroom, the children's room needs to be comfortable and somewhere that nurtures their developing personality and spirit.

THE RIGHT ATMOSPHERE

If the room looks chaotic, your children's behavior and schoolwork may mirror this, with difficulty in focusing on projects, and failure to

Toys that are left scattered around the bedroom will make your children feel unsettled and restless. Tidy soft toys away in hanging storage bags or handy soft baskets, such as these (above).

CHILDREN'S BEDROOM CLUTTER CHECKLIST

Go through the room with your children, sorting out their toys and other equipment according to the five-bag system (see page 31).

◆ Toys and games: throw away everything that is broken and give away the unwanted or discarded items.

◆ Books: reserve the favorites and give away old titles to deserving recipients such as hospitals.

◆ Computer games: see if you can sell or exchange the ones that have fallen from favor.

◆ Clothes: appraise clothes that are actually worn and pass on ones that are too small to younger children.

achieve the grades of which they are capable. The room's energy will also seem heavy, making them listless and lacking in enthusiasm.

If your children are sleeping in bunk beds, move them to separate beds as soon as you can, as the child on the bottom can feel restricted or compressed. In a teenager's room, a computer should be screened off so that its yang energies don't affect sleep. Avoid having a television in the bedroom, but if there is one, make sure it does not face the bed, and unplug it at night to reduce electromagnetic stress.

COLOR, MOOD, AND LIGHTING

Most children react strongly to color. Bright colors and busy wallpaper designs can look good, but may be too stimulating for active children; soft pastel colors, purples, blues, and greens will calm them. Give quieter children a

A chaotic bedroom (left, below) can give children problems with sleeping. Storage in bright primary colors (above) is always appealing and works well with children who are not too active. Pull-down blinds can conceal larger toys.

boost with pinks or oranges, and encourage creative children to thrive with shades of yellow.

Bedroom lighting is normally soft and ambient, but because of the mixed activities in children's rooms, good task lighting is important. Place a desk lamp in the study area, and install a sufficiently bright bedside lamp for reading as young eyes can strain easily.

Fabric or paper mobiles hung near the cot or bed, but not over it, are very relaxing for babies and toddlers. Restrict teenagers from having a vast collection of action-packed or violent posters, as they are too stimulating.

Stored benefits

Once you and your children have battled over their possessions, glance around their bedroom and see where you can create more storage. Don't forget that hanging units take up very little space. As this is a multi-activity room, for sleep and play, you need to leave clear floor space so that positive chi can move freely through it .

Ingenious canvas hanging racks with numerous pockets can hold tiny toys and small pieces of clothing.

Painting a storage unit in a bright color with a stencilled pattern can make it blend into the background.

STORAGE SOLUTIONS

Toys and games Children always have their favorites, so make sure that these are readily available. Try to get children to tidy up every night, explaining that they will feel better if they do so. Wooden chests or blanket-style boxes will hold soft toys. Transparent or colorful plastic stacking boxes, which can stand on the floor or sit in a wooden unit, are great for building blocks and small plastic toys. Fabric-covered boxes with lids are also useful and will stack on top of each other. For toy soldiers and other very small items, wooden units with several shallow drawers are ideal.

Canvas or cotton hanging bags, suspended from hooks on the wall or closets, will hold miscellaneous items. Games, which are more bulky, are best stacked on to wooden or metal shelf units.

Books Keeping too many books in the bedroom can be over-stimulating, so try and persuade your children to retain a select few here, and stow these neatly on bookshelves.

Computer games, disks, software, and CDs This modern form of clutter is particularly prevalent in teenagers' rooms. It is hard to get teenagers to be tidy, but persuade them to stash disks and CDs in plastic boxes or on bookshelves, and put software disks and computer-related manuals out of sight in closets or on shelves.

Clothes and shoes Brightly patterned cotton hanging units hold several pairs of young children's shoes. For older children and teenagers, tiered shoe racks or hanging canvas or mesh racks fit inside closets (see page 37). If you are replanning the room, think about installing closets with good hanging space and several shelves so that sweatshirts, T-shirts, sweaters, and other items can be piled here, perhaps within pull-out plastic boxes. Again, make the most of hanging space with multiple skirt and pants hangers (see page 37).

Discourage children from leaving clothes on the floor at night. Clothes should be hung up, or placed in a canvas sack or laundry hamper.

Bright plastic storage boxes on wheels hold a lot and can be easily moved around the bedroom. Do not store them under the bed regularly, as this can cause disturbed sleep.

A Nurturing Place

Often considered the "heart" of the home, the kitchen is where the family gather to eat, catch up on news, and relax. It should be a warm and cozy environment, where everyone feels cocooned by its comforting ambience, and where senses are stimulated by wonderful, aromatic cooking smells.

The kitchen has become a room of many other functions, too: children do their homework, adults steal half an hour to read a newspaper, and friends drop by, drawn by the welcoming atmosphere. And because this is where the family is fed and nurtured, the energy that moves through it needs to be positive. Cluttered counter tops, refrigerator, freezer, cabinets, and floors will block chi flow, preventing the balance and harmony required there.

THE ENERGY TRAPS

If you can never find that spice jar or bag of flour that you want because your cabinets are overstocked, or if you are constantly searching for the right kitchen accessory on your crowded counters, a good clear-out is well overdue.

Good feelings of warmth and contentment should abound in a kitchen area. Keeping counters clear and having enough shelving and kitchen units will promote a good flow of energy.

ENERGY GRIDLOCK

Chi comes into a crowded kitchen and its progress towards the window is hindered by too much stored on counters, a full trash can and full sink. The smooth movement of chi through the window to the door is stopped by crowded shelves and a messy floor.

ENERGY FREEWAY

Chi flows easily into a tidy kitchen, around cleared garbage over a clean sink and out of window. Chi comes in the window and freely moves over neat shelves, around an ordered trash can and tidied floor, and out of the door.

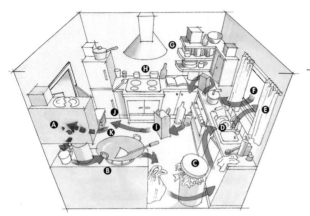

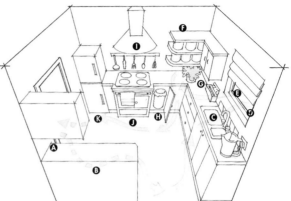

KEY: A chi enters; B overstacked cabinets; C overflowing trash can; D cluttered sink; E chi leaves; F chi comes in window; G overladen shelves; H crowded counters; I littered floor; J newspapers; K chi leaves.

KEY: A chi enters; B cleared cabinets; C empty sink; D chi leaves room; E chi comes in window; F structured shelves; G energizing plant; H empty, hidden trash can; I hanging utensils; J empty floor; K chi leaves.

Kitchen cabinets Overloading these will create a very oppressive atmosphere. Check use-by dates of packaged goods — if they have expired, you are allowing negative energies to enter this area. Stale energy is also created by unwanted or cracked dishes and glasses.

Work surfaces If you fill your counter tops with too many utensils, gadgets, storage jars, and other kitchen items, chi will be slowed down and this can adversely affect how you feel when cooking and eating in the kitchen.

Garbage cans An overflowing trash can creates negative energy and will seriously block energy flow, so empty it regularly.

Refrigerators and freezers These should always be full of food to symbolize the family's good health and wealth, but again, keep an eye on use-by dates, because storing expired goods could be very detrimental to the family's welfare.

Appliances Positive energy is given off by electrical equipment in the kitchen, but if broken appliances are left to fester on counters, they will bring about energy blockages that will affect the room's happy atmosphere.

Floor area Bottles, newspapers, and other items stacked haphazardly on the kitchen floor will look untidy and also make the flow of chi very sluggish.

A place of nourishment

Removing food that is no longer fresh from the kitchen, and getting appliances mended will make you feel better (see checklist), but you'll need to tune in to the atmosphere, too. Do you like the room, and does its energy embrace you? Or do you feel irritation because its counter tops are cluttered and your cabinets are a mess?

Crowding too much kitchenware on open shelves (above) creates distraction and disturbance, so clear out what's not needed and display attractive glasses, crockery and storage jars (left).

FEED THE ATMOSPHERE

If your cabinets contain enough packaged goods to keep you going for years, then you are missing out on the nurturing environment your family needs. Why are you hoarding so much food – are you worried subconsciously that you will not have enough? Does it stem from a childhood where food was restricted? Try to keep a sensible stockpile. Inspect the stove – if the burners are dirty, you will restrict positive Fire energy, reduce the benefit you get from your food, and maybe inhibit your wealth potential. If the oven is positioned right next to the sink, refrigerator, or freezer, a conflict between Fire and Water occurs, which will disrupt the atmosphere of the room. Avoid this by placing a wood or metal unit between them to create a barrier. If your kitchen table is under an overhead beam, it will be affected by downward "cutting" chi, which is bad feng shui. This cutting chi also affects tables that are close to sharp corners, which can prove harmful. Both can cause conflict at mealtimes, so move the table away from the beam and block cutting chi with plants.

COLOR, MOOD, AND LIGHTING

A kitchen needs to be airy and inviting, so white works well here – to the Chinese, this symbolizes purity. The ideal kitchen location is in the east or southeast sector of the house (Wood), so if yours faces in this direction you can enhance it with shades of green (Wood) or blue (Water), because Water produces Wood in the element cycle. Wooden flooring and cabinets add natural warmth.

Be careful not to use a strong red in a south-facing (Fire) kitchen, because it will emphasize the element too strongly, although white and metal accessories can counter this.

Good lighting brings in positive yang energy, so add downlighters or spotlights, and use strip lighting under units to illuminate food preparation areas

Messy sinks, overflowing trash cans and other garbage upsets the harmony in the kitchen (above). Concealing trash in a unit and storing other kitchen goods away neatly will make the room seem calm but inviting. White is a good kitchen color as it symbolizes purity (left).

Streamlined stocks

If you're suffering from exhaustion, having ruthlessly gone through the kitchen evaluating what you really do and do not need, take a short break to think about how you can increase your storage options for all the items that are left. See if you have space for more cabinets, shelves, or wall units.

STORAGE SOLUTIONS

Packaged goods and canned food

If your canned and packaged goods are still too numerous to store in cabinets, consider adding extra units. Narrow cabinets can take advantage of a small gap.

Dishes and glasses Make a feature of these by displaying them in an open-fronted cabinet in a kitchen or dining area. Pine or painted cabinets with glass doors also do the job.

Fruit and vegetables A good way of storing these quickly-consumed foods is to pack them in plastic baskets, and push these into either an open-fronted or closed cabinet under a kitchen counter. Wicker baskets also look good used individually or when stacked together and slid under counters. When space is tight, fresh produce can be placed in metal mesh baskets hung from a hook in the wall or the ceiling. Alternatively, a cart with basket shelves is useful because it can be wheeled out of sight quickly.

Cleaning goods All too often these disappear into a dark jungle under the sink, and it's difficult to identify what's living there. One solution is to fit a wire container with different compartments that slide in and out. You could also put the items into different baskets or plastic boxes and stack them on shelves under the sink.

Utensils and gadgets On kitchen counters, keep these to a minimum. House sharp knives in cutlery units or wooden knife blocks. Never hang knives on a magnetic rack, because the sharp points will create harmful cutting chi. Other utensils can be suspended from strong hooks on a rail, possibly positioned above the stove. Pans and cups can also be taken from cabinets and hung from rails if you have limited storage space.

Miscellaneous items A kitchen cart is a useful object and can sit under a counter or at the side of the kitchen when not in use. Its tiled or wooden top gives you an extra preparation surface, while bottles of wine, regularly used dishes, utensils, or drying cloths can be stored on the bottom. Many contain drawers or handy hanging rails.

Storage jars, preserves, and pasta jars These are good candidates for display, so clear them from counter tops and place on simple open shelves. You can put up narrow shelves or racks to hold all your spices, making them easily accessible, which will also liberate some space in your cabinets.

Electrical appliances Only leave out the appliances that you use regularly, such as the toaster and coffee machine. Store any other items like the iron, liquidizer, juicer, and food processor in deep drawer units, or in cabinets with deep shelves.

KITCHEN CLUTTER CHECKLIST

Go through all your cabinets, sorting out items according to the five-bag system (see page 31).

◆ Packaged goods, sauces, and cans of food: check for stale goods and those past their use-by date and throw out.

◆ Bottles, newspapers, old cartons, and carrier bags: recycle these items, and take to the recycling center regularly. Keep plastic bags for re-use.

◆ Appliances: if an appliance is broken, get it fixed or get rid of it.

◆ Trash cans: try to empty these daily, as they breed stagnancy in an otherwise positive area.

◆ Under the sink: assess cleaning products and materials and only keep those you use regularly – get rid of impulse buys that have never been used.

◆ Refrigerator and freezer: check each shelf, removing items that aren't fresh and out-of-date products.

◆ Counter tops: minimize utensils and recycle glass storage jars.

When you have thrown out the kitchen goods that are not needed, display pleasing products such as storage jars, vinegars, and oils on open shelving.

The "Mouth" of the Home

The front entrance and hall of your home are the first places friends and visitors see when they call around. It reflects your personality – a place of joyous welcomes and sad farewells. From here, you view the world from both the inside and outside. The hall should be bright and welcoming – an area that invites people in.

ENERGY GRIDLOCK

Chi comes through the front door, is obstructed by objects behind the door and is prevented from moving up the stairs by blockages. Chi going down the hall is restricted by too many items and a bulging closet.

KEY: A chi enters; B boxes and shopping cart; C notes on mirror; D chi goes up stairs; E obstacles on stairs; F chi goes down hall; G overladen coat rack; H bike and other clutter; I closet full of junk; J chi leaves.

Chi, the beneficial energy that creates balance and harmony, enters through the front door – the "mouth" of the home – fulfiling the same function as food entering our bodies. Chi needs to flow in strongly and positively without obstruction, so cut back any overgrown plants or trees around the doorway, because they will inhibit its movement. If, once chi enters the home, it has to struggle around items such as boxes, strollers, and an overflowing coat rack, the symbolic meaning of this is that you are finding life hard work.

ENERGY FREEWAY

Chi meanders into an ordered home, is slowed by a wind-chime and moves effortlessly around a storage unit and clean mirror and up well-lit, cleared stairs. Chi going down the hall flows around a neat coat rack and umbrella stand along the empty floor, past plant which slows chi, and an ordered closet.

KEY: A chi enters; B put wind chime over door; C storage unit and key holder; D mirror; E well-lit, inspirational pictures; F cleared stairs; G chi goes down hall; H organized coat rack; I healthy plant; J empty floor; K rationalized closet; L chi leaves.

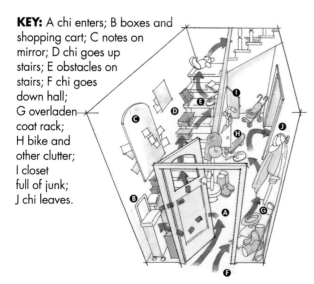

The hall is the first place that visitors see when they enter your home, so it needs to be uncluttered with a bright and inviting atmosphere and good lighting.

THE ENERGY TRAPS

An overcrowded hall, where everybody sees fit to leave miscellaneous items scattered haphazardly all over the floor, will soon start to wear you down. You may feel your life is losing direction, and, because chi can't enter this area properly, you will be restricted in everything you are trying to do, and new opportunities will be blocked.

The porch and hall Tripping over old umbrellas, golf clubs, bikes, stroller, random boxes, muddy shoes or boots will cause constant annoyance and irritation. The hampered flow of chi will disturb the atmosphere, making visitors feel uneasy as they enter your home.

Hall table or desk Stacks of local newspapers, junk mail, and unpaid bills are stale energy and this will slow down your progress in life.

Alcoves These are dangerously shaped for attracting clutter and so forming negative energies – beware!

Stairs If you leave files, books, and papers on the stairs, you will restrict the energy flow through the home and feel a heaviness every time you go upstairs.

Under the stairs If this is your "black hole" where every possible item of junk is stored, its stale energy will seep out into other areas of your home. This can make the people who live there feel lethargic and depressed.

HALL CLUTTER CHECKLIST

Decide what to keep and what to throw away, making piles to put into your five-bag system (see page 31).

◆ Shoes, boots: return to the closet, or to the garbage if they are worn out.

◆ Junk mail, newspapers, bills, keys: sort through the piles, then file the essentials and recycle or dispense with the rest.

◆ Coat rack: check through all the jackets and coats, decide what is currently used, and throw away or store the remainder elsewhere.

◆ Bikes, strollers, golf clubs, sports gear: if these are not being used, sell or give them away; alternatively, find good storage solutions.

◆ Home repair items: get rid of dried-up paint, old glue, and other out-of-date products that may be lurking under the stairs.

The inner world

Removing obstructions from your hall and entrance will help you to move on in life (see checklist), but also study its overall atmosphere. Is it bright and inviting, or dark and restricting? Does it echo how you feel about your life?

HALL LAYOUT PROBLEMS

If your entrance and hall are a mess, ask yourself why you are stopping good things coming into your life. See how your door opens – does it get blocked by clutter inhibiting the chi? Look at the geography of the area. According to feng shui, the stairs should not start directly opposite the main door, and a curved staircase is often preferable to one that is straight. If your stairs do face the door, hanging wind chimes over the front door will help slow down the flow of energy.

COLOR, MOOD, AND LIGHTING

A warm, welcoming light outside and good ceiling lighting inside will encourage people in. To expand a narrow hall, hang a mirror on a side wall. To lead people to the first floor, put up well-lit inspirational pictures along the stairs. As this area should be welcoming, soft pastel blues, greens, pinks, or shades of white or cream are soothing colors for walls and paintwork.

Left: Shades of white or soft pastels can help to expand a narrow hall. This area need not be stark; when you have removed any clutter, hang inspiring pictures, fit interesting lights and add chairs, tables, or small storage cabinets.

Left: Too many coats, jackets and scarves can overwhelm coat racks, so give away those you don't need and choose a functional style that works for you and your family.

STORAGE SOLUTIONS

After your major clear-out, muse about new storage solutions that will blend with the pleasant ambience of this area.

Shoes and boots A tiered plastic or metal shoe rack in the porch or by the front door will hold several pairs of shoes. Alternatively, install neat wooden shoe cabinets with hinged drawers in the hall, or a tall, slim cabinet that combines sloping shelves for shoes at the bottom with other useful shelves above.

Hats, coats, and jackets Choose a coat rack with a rail or bars from which to hang items, and a flat area on top for hats, gloves, and scarves. Or, place a conventional coat stand in an unused corner. There are also units with outer hooks for jackets, and sliding doors concealing shelves for shoes.

Junk mail, bills, and keys A desk or low wooden storage unit with drawers can house these items. Hang keys on the wall behind for easy access. Clip interesting flyers together and file in drawers or cardboard magazine files. Put bills in a plastic folder with compartments.

Bikes, strollers, sports equipment, and home repair items Preferably, store bikes in a garage or shed, or under the stairs. Suspend the stroller from a strong hook under the stairs or in a hall closet; likewise, hang golf clubs and sports equipment. There are special under-the-stair units for open staircases, with different-sized plastic stacking units. These are ideal for storing home repair paraphernalia.

Sociability and Relaxation

he living room is the focal point of the home, where the family gathers to unwind from the relentless pressures of daily life. It is a room where lively conversations about the state of the country or the meaning of life can stretch long into the night. It is a special meeting place, where old and new guests are welcomed and entertained.

The living room is often multifunctional, with one area for relaxing, another for dining, and

A well-planned seating layout in your living room adds to its appeal and conviviality. Making sure it is junk-free will aid energy movement and sociability.

a corner for a home office, from which the household is run and organized.

Although this is essentially a tranquil room, the living room is also a sociable place and needs a positive chi movement in order to keep

ENERGY GRIDLOCK

Chi streams into the crowded living room to the window, hitting videos on the floor and struggling around a piled bookcase and coffee table. It is slowed by clutter behind the sofa, boxes of wine and a muddled cupboard. From the window to its exit through the door it is restricted by the crowded table, furniture and floor.

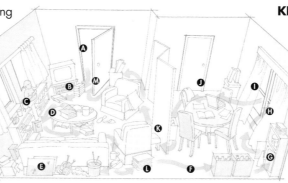

KEY: A chi enters; B piles of videos; C overstacked bookcase; D messy coffee table; E piles of junk and CDs; F unwanted boxes; G too full unit; H chi leaves; I chi comes in window; J untidy table; K jumbled floor; L mess behind furniture; M chi leaves.

conversations flowing and to create a good, uplifting ambience. If the room is cluttered or over-furnished, the energy will stagnate, engendering an unsettled and restless atmosphere, rather than the desired feeling of contentment and relaxation.

THE ENERGY TRAPS

Finding a big piece of furniture barring your way when you enter your living room, or having to navigate around piles of newspapers, magazines, and other paraphernalia, is at odds with the aim of creating a relaxing, sociable ambience, so you need to do some clearing and streamlining.

Behind sofas Your sofa can be a clutter magnet. If the area behind your sofa conceals discarded craft projects, unhung pictures, useless leaflets, and packages of old photographs, then you have created a brooding stagnancy behind you that will disturb you every time you sit down.

On bookshelves Symbolically, books are linked to your likes and beliefs, so if there are a lot of dusty old books sitting on the shelves, it indicates that you are becoming very set in your ways.

Overcrowded mantles A vast assortment of ornaments, candlesticks, dishes, and ashtrays looks unsightly and will induce a restless energy.

ENERGY FREEWAY

Chi enters the well-planned lounge, sweeping around the re-vamped TV storage unit and bookcase with plant, around the empty coffee table and tidied furniture and floor to the cleared unit and out of the window. The chi that enters by the window streams over the polished table, over the clean floor and out of the door.

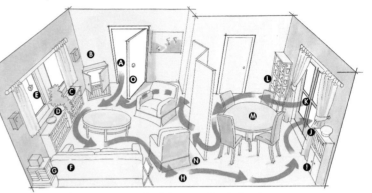

KEY: A chi enters; B stacked TV unit; C tidy bookcase; D energizing plant; E hanging crystal to slow energy; F cleared furniture; G CD unit; H bare floor; I organized unit; J chi leaves; K chi enters; L extra storage unit; M empty table; N cleared floor; O chi leaves.

Under coffee tables Overflowing piles of magazines will bring about a central area of stale energy that will slow down all the family.

Overstocked cabinets or storage units Stacks of old videos, records, CDs, cassette tapes, and other items, piled haphazardly on top of each other, link you too much to your past, rather than your future. Chi will be very sluggish here, and actually make people reluctant to play music at all.

Bar If, when you open the door, the first thing that you see is odd, cracked glasses and almost empty bottles of alcohol, the mess and disorder will bring you down.

The comfort zone

Getting down to the task of refining your main living space and making it more comfortable is very rewarding, but before you start your clear-out (see checklist), take some time out to assess this area where you spend so much of your time, to see what it says about you. Does its décor and furnishings welcome you, or are they looking tired and shabby, perhaps reflecting what you are secretly feeling about your life? Are you keeping it cluttered and overcrowded as a kind of sign that you are refusing to let changes happen in your life?

ROOM TO RELAX?

A cluttered living room will deter guests from lingering. If your room is like this, it may reveal a subconscious desire to keep people away.

Pay attention to the positioning of furniture. Sofas and chairs are best placed in a semi-circle around a coffee table or in front of the fire so that they face each other, making it easy for

It is hard to relax in a room which is full of unloved and discarded items (left). Keep as little as possible on coffee tables (above) and display your favorite, loved possessions on attractive storage units.

Regularly go through your books and review what you really need as too many old ones can make you set in your ways (left). Place your favorite books and treasured artefacts that are left on well-lit shelving (below).

people to chat. Never put chairs under a ceiling beam, because the cutting chi that comes down from it can cause headaches. Sharp edges and pointed structures create bad feng shui and are referred to as poison arrows. To avoid your suffering from the effects of these, furniture such as shelves with sharp edges can be obscured with trailing plants, while sharp-angled tables can be covered with interesting fabrics. In a large living area, a dining area can be demarcated with shelving units or large sofas.

COLOR, MOOD, AND LIGHTING

Shades of cream or soft pastel colors create a relaxing ambience. Yellow will expand a room and helps to stimulate conversation.

Alternatively, you can paint the room in a color that relates to the room's element according to the Pa Kua. So, if it faces north, for example, it should be blue, but if it faces south, a shade of red is appropriate (see page 14).

Lighting draws in good yang energy. Use uplighters or pendant lights for background lighting, lamps for mood lighting, and spotlights for accent lighting on pictures, ornaments, and plants. The soft light of candles adds a special appeal. To promote feelings of wellbeing and harmony, burn fragrant incense or essential oils.

Structured tranquility

Clearing out items from this room is never easy, but you will immediately notice a lightening of its atmosphere when you do so. Walk around the room and decide how you can improve the storage of your remaining possessions. If you adore books and still have many left, appraise where you might fit another shelving unit.

STORAGE SOLUTIONS

Books Consider building shelves into any unused alcoves. You can also position a cabinet there to hold other miscellaneous goods. A wide, freestanding open wooden bookcase will hold many titles. Try to intersperse sections of books with ornaments to break up the solidity of its appearance. Buy a bookcase on rollers so that it can be moved around easily, or used as a room divider for separating dining and relaxation areas.

Take your CDs off the floor and house them in stylish wooden cabinets such as this one.

LIVING ROOM CLUTTER CHECKLIST

Work methodically through your living room items, making distinct piles to put into your five-bag system (see page 31).

◆ Books: be ruthless – keep the special ones, but sell the rest or give to thrift stores or a hospital.

◆ Loose photographs: these create dull energy, so sort through them all and put the pictures that give you joy into frames or an album, then discard the rest.

◆ Magazines and newspapers: cut out interesting articles and keep for reference, then take the rest to a recycling center.

◆ Old videos, records, CDs, and cassette tapes: sell what you can, and discard any old tapes.

◆ Trinkets: ask yourself why you are keeping gifts or old family handowns that you don't like. Retain only those that you really love and give away the rest.

◆ Glasses, bottles of alcohol: glasses create positive energy, but not if damaged. Throw out those that are cracked or chipped, and discard bottles that are almost empty.

Photographs Go through these carefully, only keeping those that fill you with love and affection. The danger of hoarding a vast collection of old photographs is that it can link you too strongly to your past. Just keep a few happy pictures of past relationships and dispense with the rest. Make a montage in a glass clipframe of current photos of family and friends. Or display photos of loved ones or happy vacations in metal or wood frames in your relationship or fame areas respectively (see pages 14–15). Place all other pictures in albums and store neatly in a cabinet or drawer.

Magazines and newspapers These form an ongoing clutter problem that needs constant vigilance. Once you have cut out any articles you want for reference, keep current newspapers and magazines in a stylish magazine rack made from metal, wood, or other combinations. One ingenious cast-iron model has hooped sides so that newspapers can be stored flat, and string may be tied round them for easy removal to a recycling center.

TV, videotapes, CDs, and cassette tapes Easy access is the key for these frequently used items. Feng shui practice dictates that it is preferable to cover a television when it is not in use, as it gives off so much yang energy and

electromagnetic stress, so house it in a cabinet or TV unit with doors. Videotapes can be stored in a bottom drawer. CD units are available in different styles to blend in with your room's décor; wider units will hold up to 244 CDs. Freestanding metal shelving units are also a good solution for CDs and videotapes.

Trinkets Place on shelves with books, or display a favored collection in an illuminated glass cabinet. Clever small cube units (open, with doors, or including shelves) can be mixed and matched to display trinkets, vases, favorite books and picture frames.

Glasses and bottles Glasses are very yang and add to the positive energy of the living room. Good-quality glassware looks stunning arranged in a glass cabinet with a wooden frame. Inbuilt downlighters really high-light the sparkle of the glasses.

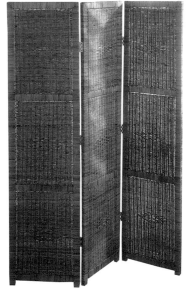

Soft baskets can hold craft projects (left). Screens can divide multifunctional rooms (above). Candles add yang energy to the living room (right).

Purifying the Soul

Bathrooms are places where we can escape from the world, so need to be tranquil rooms with clear floors and surfaces.

S oaking in a hot, relaxing bath or reviving yourself with a quick shower can help you forget all the problems of the day. The bathroom is a place where you can close the door and escape from the outside world – a private retreat for cleansing the body and soul, and somewhere for meditation, contemplation, and inspiration, where ideas are considered and new ones are born. It needs to be a warm and inviting environment where you want to linger – a place that cherishes you.

In a bathroom, water is constantly draining away, making it a very yin environment that is prone to stagnation. A surfeit of furniture and messy, overcrowded surfaces will slow down chi energy and stop it circulating properly. The ensuing atmosphere will be stale and the room will make you feel restless and unsettled. In feng

ENERGY GRIDLOCK

Chi comes into the cluttered bathroom and is blocked by boxes of bathroom products, it then hits the crowded vanity unit and medicine cabinet and is further hindered by clothes on the floor and the mass of beauty items around the bath before it goes out of the window. The flow of chi from the window is interrupted by more products on the bath and towels on the floor before it exits the room.

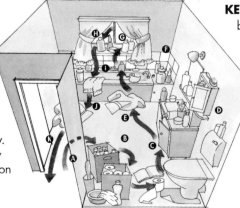

KEY: A chi enters; B boxes of bathroom products; C crowded vanity unit; D overstocked medicine cabinet; E clothes on floor; F overladen bath; G chi leaves; H chi comes in window; I too many bath products; J wet towels; K chi leaves.

ENERGY FREEWAY

Chi drifts into the well-planned bathroom and around the wicker storage unit and healthy plant, over the bare floor past the overhauled vanity unit and medicine chest. It goes past an enhancing plant and candles, and out of the window. Chi flowing through the window moves fluently over the smooth bath surfaces, over the mat and towel rail and exits out of the door.

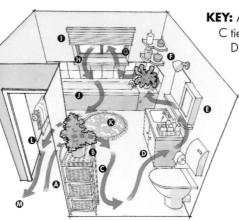

KEY: A chi enters; B energizing plant; C tiered, natural bathroom unit; D re-worked vanity unit; E cleared medicine chest; F plant and candles for yang energy; G chi leaves; H chi comes in window; I natural blind; J products moved from bath; K cotton bathmat; L heated towel rail; M chi leaves.

shui terms, bathrooms are not always viewed auspiciously, because water is also linked to money, and this room sees it running away. It is therefore preferable that it is not located in your wealth or career sector. However, they can still be pleasant environments.

THE ENERGY TRAPS

If you find it hard to get in and out of your bathroom because of all the units and baskets, or if you can never find your shampoo, conditioner, or soap because they are always buried under a mound of other toiletries, you need a thorough cleansing session.

Bathroom cabinets and vanity units

These are good for storage, but if they are packed full of beauty and bathroom items that constantly spill out when you open the doors,

making it hard to find what you want to use, you will feel irritated and frustrated.

Around the sink and side of the bath

A plethora of bottles and tubes, which are guilty of leaving messy deposits in these areas, create a chaotic, disordered feel in a room that should be pleasant and calm. Consider why you feel you need so many.

On the floor Keeping a stock of toilet paper and cleansers can be a good idea, but if they are stacked on the floor so that you constantly trip over them, they will cause annoyance.

Medicine cabinets Most medicines, tablets, and creams have a short shelf-life, so check your cabinet to ensure that you don't have expired items. Don't keep a lot of unnecessary products that are rarely used – if you do, ask yourself why you are holding onto so many products that only link to ill-health.

A haven of peace

Removing superfluous goods from your bathroom will make you feel better (see checklist), but take a few moments to get a sense of the room that you normally take for granted. It mirrors part of your personality, so do you like what you see? If the paintwork is dirty or peeling, it may indicate a pattern of neglect that you are repeating in your life. Or does its disorder suggest that you are discontented with life?

CREATING AN OASIS

Your bathroom should be an oasis where you can refresh body and mind, but if it is a mess, the chi (which is low here anyway) will struggle to work its way through. The stagnancy will drain your energy levels, making you feel constantly tired, listless, and lacking in enthusiasm for life.

COLOR, MOOD, AND LIGHTING

Bathrooms are relaxing rooms, but they do need to be fed with positive energy in order to counteract the damp, humid, slightly negative

A bathroom cabinet which is packed full of bathroom products will always irritate you as you won't be able to find anything (left). Regularly remove what you don't need from the cabinet and maybe use baskets inside to maximize the space (below). Painting the bathroom green is calming and helps aid digestion.

atmosphere that is always present. The color on the walls will also influence your mood. A soft green in a bathroom can aid digestion, while blue, linked to flowing rivers, seas, and lakes, is said to keep the water in the room flowing

BATHROOM CLUTTER CHECKLIST

Make your bathroom an enjoyable place to be by forming your five bags of clutter (see page 31).

◆ Medicines: check all the use-by dates and throw out accordingly.

◆ Bathroom cleaners, toilet paper: don't keep a year's worth out, just have a few extra rolls on hand and store your back-up collection elsewhere.

◆ Bath salts, oils, shower gels, shampoos, and conditioners: are you hoarding a lot of samples? Start working through them, or throw them away. Get rid of any products that are old, dried up or nearly used up.

◆ Towels and bath mats: do you have more sets than you need? Are they torn, fraying or have they seen better days? If so, you know what to do.

swiftly, which is beneficial. Pinks and peaches are calming and soothing.

Healthy, round-leaved plants will lift the room, while using fragrant bath lotions or burning essential oil will clear negativity. Mirrors bring in powerful energy, so position one over the sink, and keep it clean and shining. If it is tarnished or cracked, replace immediately as this is bad feng

shui and you may be adversely affected.

Soft, fluffy towels in pastel colors will counteract the harder lines of tiled surfaces and the ceramic finishes of the bath, sink, and toilet.

Ceiling downlighters, and task lighting for shaving or applying make-up, will give the right level of brightness. Use scented candles in wall sconces, or safely positioned around the bath to bring in enticing Fire energy.

Leaving wet towels and dirty clothes around the bathroom will further stagnate the slow energy here (above). This bathroom cabinet (left) can take towels, mats, or a small laundry hamper and smaller accessories in the drawers.

Perfect serenity

After you have swept through your bathroom and eliminated everything that's past its prime, rethink the way you can best display and store all the essentials in this special room. Bathrooms are often littered with an assortment of bottles of various types of scented gunk, which tend to congregate untidily on window and bath ledges. The bathroom is often humid and steamy, slowing chi flow, so aim to keep surfaces clear so that the movement of chi is not hindered further.

Towels are better placed in a unit but can be presented on shelves when clean and dry.

STORAGE SOLUTIONS
Bath and beauty products

Generally, these are very attractively packaged, so they look good on open shelving. But do not have too many products on show, just the ones that you regularly use. You can get hanging units to suspend from the shower, which hold shampoo, shower gel, sponges, and soap. Other styles have suction cups that stick to wall tiles. Metal hanging baskets, particularly in a verdigris style, can look stylish. Fit corner shelving into spaces that wouldn't otherwise be used. Glass shelves looks good, and are practical and easy to clean.

If you put on your make-up in the bathroom, consider buying a unit with drawers that incorporate divided trays with sections for brushes, foundation, lipsticks, and eyeshadows.

Medicines and first-aid kit

These are best hidden away neatly in a medicine cabinet. Alternatively, use stacking baskets in a cupboard, or tiered wicker units with pull-out drawers (good for tight spaces).

Bathroom cleansers and other products

While these are all very necessary, and you may want them on hand rather than in the kitchen, they clutter and detract from the

bathroom if they are left on view. If you lack space to store them, consider buying a vanity unit to fit under the sink. This will utilize the wasted space under the basin and give you at least two extra shelves for storing bulky items such as toilet paper, cloths, bleach, disinfectant, and bathroom cleaners.

Towels and bathmats Fluffy towels and accessories add a wonderful yin quality to the

In a large bathroom area, build in as many storage cupboards as you can so that you don't have to leave many goods out. Flowers or plants can raise the chi here.

bathroom. As they are so tactile, extra towels can be set out on display – particularly on glass shelves. Alternatively, they can be stored in glass-fronted units, or in plastic baskets set in open modern chrome units, and even mixed in with other baskets of products (see above).

Creativity and Prosperity

Most of us spend more hours each day in an office environment than we do in our own homes. Even if we work from home, we usually shut the door on our outer family world so that we can get down to work. It is here that we give full rein to our talents for bringing wealth, prosperity, and success into our lives. Clarity and concentration are essential for making the right decisions; we are constantly performing, juggling time and budgets. Here, appraisal is constant – all the efforts we make are judged and assessed by bosses, co-workers, and clients.

So, the room you work in should nurture you and your abilities – it should be a pleasant, well-lit, inspiring environment that makes you feel at ease and determined to achieve your best.

The flow of chi in an office must be strong and yang to encourage a positive attitude. If your desk is cluttered with numerous items and the floor is covered with boxes, reports, and files, chi will get stuck and your creativity and decision-making skills will be blocked, causing you to work in a confused, disorganized way.

An ordered office environment will help you think clearly and make decisions more easily.

THE ENERGY TRAPS

As well as slowing down the chi, an overcrowded office area will restrict the pace of the business, causing upsets and misunderstandings about current workloads.

The desk Stacks of paperwork awaiting action, files that have not been put away, and unpaid invoices create pools of stagnant energy, making you feel stressed, out of control, and unproductive. If you can never find anything you need in your desk drawers because they are full of irrelevant office equipment, pens that don't work, and old notes, this confusion will make you work sluggishly.

Filing cabinets When these are overfilled with redundant projects or contain information about bad clients, they create a negative space in the office.

Floor area If it is an obstacle course of boxes, stacks of files, old reports, printer paper, and other items, these will all restrict energy flow, making the office atmosphere dull.

Cabinets Bulging office cabinets can make people feel oppressed and threatened.

Shelves Out-of-date reference books, catalogs or brochures just link the business to its past.

Computer Leaving old material on your machine will hold you back from progressing with new projects.

ENERGY GRIDLOCK

Chi proceeds into the jumbled office and is stopped by an overflowing trash can, files, and a full filing cabinet. It tries to move over a littered desk and window ledge before escaping out of the window. Chi streaming in through the window is restricted by too many books on the fax unit and boxes on floor before leaving the room.

ENERGY FREEWAY

Chi moves into a spring-cleaned office and works easily around emptied filing cabinet and stored files, over the ordered desk space and window ledge and out of the window. The flow of chi back through the window is encouraged by a healthy plant, an uncluttered fax unit and an empty floor area before leaving the room.

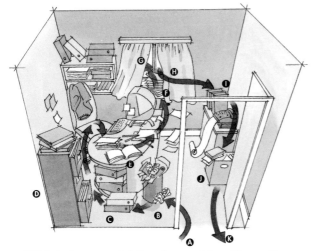

KEY: A chi enters; B full trash can; C box files on floor; D groaning filing cabinet; E disorganized desk; F piles of paperwork; G chi leaves; H chi comes in window; I stacks of books; J crowded box; K chi leaves

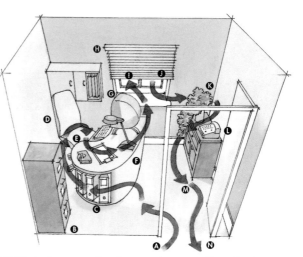

KEY: A chi enters; B cabinet with current files; C tidy box files; D supportive chair; E efficient desk space; F task light; G clear window ledge; H wooden blind; I chi leaves; J chi enters; K plant to boost atmosphere; L tidy fax unit, M cleared floor; N chi leaves

The work domain

Going through an office and throwing out what's not needed is hard work (see checklist), so first take a few moments to view your working environment through different eyes. Does it make you feel claustrophobic? Do you feel happy working there, and does its color and lighting work well, lifting your energy?

WORK ETHICS

To help you work well, the room's atmosphere must encourage productivity. Does the atmosphere feel slow and heavy? If so, it may be a reflection of a business that is run in a rather haphazard way. Consider how your business or company is doing. Has new work decreased or have orders dropped? A disorganized office will dramatically affect the smooth running of a business. Chi will have a problem working its way around the room, and you will feel this hindrance in everything that you attempt – people will always be engaged when you call, important appointments will be canceled, or files will suddenly go missing.

If you work at home on your own, and find that you are often restless and unable to sit still or concentrate for long during your working day, it

Files, reports, and other papers scattered on the floor will confuse your working practice, so have as many filing cabinets as you can. These Asian wooden ones are also attractive pieces of furniture.

may be because you are surrounded by clutter. Check to see if cutting chi is coming from sharp corners or shelves and hitting your desk. If so, deflect it with healthy, green, round-leaved plants, or push books to the front of shelves to soften their hard edges. Fresh flowers will lift everyone's mood and raise the energy of the office. Always remember to empty all trash cans daily so that you are not surrounded by pockets of stagnant energy.

The effects of electromagnetic stress from a computer can be alleviated by taking regular breaks and placing a clear quartz or rose quartz crystal next to it to soak up some of the negative emissions. A cactus called *Cirrus peruvianus* is also good for absorbing the emissions. Peace lilies, peperomias, and dwarf banana plants help cleanse the atmosphere.

COLOR, MOOD, AND LIGHTING

Light creams, white or pastel colors will increase the space and airiness of an office, or the room can be painted according to the appropriate element of the Pa Kua (see page 14). Good overhead lighting is important, and daylight bulbs, although expensive, help reduce eyestrain as they are the nearest to the ultraviolet light we experience outside. Angled desk lamps assist close reading and computer work.

Sunlight introduces warmth and yang energy, but can be blinding and create irritating glare on computers, even in winter, so venetian blinds on windows are essential. To reduce glare, position your desk so that windows are to one side of it. If you cannot avoid glare, hang a faceted spherical crystal (see page 90) in the window to dispel the glare's negative chi.

In a home office, ideally face south as this is your fame area. Always sit with your back to the wall, for support, and face the door.

Successful placement

The position of your desk can affect your work efficiency and achievements. The best position, in feng shui terms, is in the corner that is diagonally opposite the main door of your office. You need to be able to see the door and who is coming into the room. If you sit with your back to the door, you will always feel threatened, or that other colleagues are betraying you. However, if sitting like this is unavoidable, you can hang a small mirror over your desk so that you see the door behind you reflected in it.

Your chair should always have a solid wall, rather than a window, behind it, because this gives you symbolic support. If you have no choice but to sit with a window behind you, then keep the blind down – doing this symbolizes a measure of support. Also, avoid sitting too close to the office door, because it will make you feel that you are unprotected and that you are losing control.

Tall, slim filing cabinets can be slotted into narrow spaces in the office.

SITING A HOME OFFICE

An ideal position for your home office (if you are running a business) is facing south, because this governs your fame area. Situate a home study to face the northeast, which relates to your education and knowledge area. If these positions are not possible, use your compass (see page 15) and place your desk in a south or northeast corner.

AN OPEN-PLAN OFFICE

When several members of staff share an open-plan office, it is better to get a feng shui consultant in to map it out and ascertain the best positions for people to sit. Alternatively, use the compass and Pa Kua and from your readings work out the most auspicious areas for computers, fax machines, and filing cabinets. You can also follow some general guidelines. The most favorable position for the manager's office is farthest from the office door, so that he or she is apart from the bustle of the office, and is able to make decisions without distractions, promoting good control over the business. Do not place desks facing each other because this can cause confrontation between colleagues.

Right: If your desk is constantly in a mess, you will work in a distracted, unstructured way and will be forever losing files, invoices, and vital reports and notes. Try to address correspondence as soon as it comes in, or make your comments and pass it on. The aim at the end of the day is to leave an empty, tidy desk – this is not always easy to achieve, but it is something to aim for.

Computer disks and fiddly stationery items such as staples, paperclips, erasers, and pens and pencils can be put in this small unit (below).

OFFICE CLUTTER CHECKLIST

Although clearing out office clutter is slightly different from sorting out the home, you can still use the five-bag system (see page 31).

◆ Files: sort through your filing cabinets and throw out redundant files, keeping only the current ones.

◆ Catalogs, reference magazines, and brochures: send old ones for recycling.

◆ Reference books: keep up-to-date books with the latest information, and give the rest away.

◆ Reports: retain reference copies of old reports and shred the rest.

◆ Desk: transfer messages or Post-it notes to your diary, and junk any irrelevant pieces of paper crowding the desk.

◆ Computer: go through the hard disk and put unused programs, completed or abandoned projects, and e-mails on a back-up disk or archiving system, or throw them away.

Inspired filing

Now that you have started taking action in your home office or your place of work by removing waste and clutter, you need to evaluate how to make better use of your space so that it doesn't become a mess again. See if there is room for more filing cabinets to consume paperwork or files stacked on the floor. Is it necessary to buy another cabinet for stationery? Perhaps an alcove can be utilized by building in more shelves for reference books.

Stationery trays need not be only metal or plastic but can also be made from natural fibers, which are good for the movement of chi (left).

If you do not have many files, these storage boxes will be perfectly adequate (above).

STORAGE SOLUTIONS

Files If your company has numerous projects running at one time, with related files, it is worth installing tall, metal filing cabinets that feature several shelves of hanging files. Box files can be stored in smaller versions with deeper shelves. Alternatively, incorporate conventional metal filing cabinets with two, three, or four drawers. To boost the Metal element, place these in the west of the office. In a home office, there is usually a less pressing demand for filing space, and attractive wooden units with one filing drawer and two storage drawers will suffice. Buy one that is on rollers, so that it will slide under a desk. Some computer desk units have a pull-out keyboard shelf and extra drawers and shelves for computer accessories and manuals.

Stationery This can easily get out of control, so if your present cabinet is inadequate, invest in furniture to contain it, such as a tall metal unit with three shelves and lockable doors. Smaller cabinets with one shelf are also available. A multi-drawer cabinet can adequately hold business stationery.

Compartmentalized insert trays can be added for loose items such as paperclips, pens, and markers. For home use, stylish plastic drawer units on rollers will absorb any miscellaneous pieces of stationery. Stacking boxes in transparent plastic look good sitting on shelves, and will hold disks, CD Rom disks, and index cards.

If you are on a tight budget, these inexpensive cardboard boxes will hold different items.

Printer paper Rather than leaving stacks of paper lying on the floor, improve matters with a cabinet where the printer sits on top and paper is stored on shelves below.

Catalogs, brochures, and reports These are very messy when scattered around an office, so place in labeled box files. Store these on open metal or wooden shelving units, moving the files so that they are flush with the edges of the container to avoid creating cutting chi. They can also be secreted in stackable modular units with pull-down doors. For the home office, use transparent plastic lidded stacking boxes or plastic magazine holders to keep brochures or catalogs stored neatly.

Reference books Stand in rows on open metal or wood shelving units as above, but never position one behind a desk because it can send out cutting chi. Ideally, look for a unit with deep shelves fitted with doors to counteract this problem, or use freestanding cabinets with several shelves and glass or wooden doors.

Where Memories Live on

All too often, the attic becomes a memorial junkyard to our past. This space above us can symbolically oppress us with our past emotions – our elation at success in school or sports, our sadness at the loss of relatives, or failure in various projects. It encompasses the pain and passion of love affairs, and the pride and unconditional love of parenthood. The past spirit of the home seems to rest here, lingering over the family like a murky cloud. The attic can also be a repository for feelings of disapproval and dislike, as we secrete more and more unwanted gifts in this deep, dark space.

The flow of energy through this higher-level storage area is naturally sluggish, as there tends to be little ventilation. However, it is important that chi is able to move, and if the attic is full to the brim with junk, it will struggle to move at all, and become an inhibiting heaviness that looms continuously over the house. If your room is like this, stop and consider why you feel you need to hold on to so many reminders of your past – are you worried or frightened about what the future might hold?

THE ENERGY TRAPS

Inevitably, the attic holds many different possessions, but it is what is placed here and how it is stored is what really matters.

ENERGY GRIDLOCK

Chi flows up to the chaotic attic and is immediately stopped by piles of old boxes. It struggles sluggishly over scattered sporting equipment, boxes of old toys, boxed games, decaying picture frames, clothes, and other junk before going out the trap door.

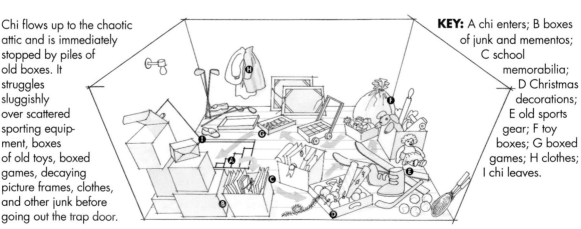

KEY: A chi enters; B boxes of junk and mementos; C school memorabilia; D Christmas decorations; E old sports gear; F toy boxes; G boxed games; H clothes; I chi leaves.

ENERGY FREEWAY

Chi travels into the overhauled attic moving freely around storage boxes, a boot rack, other boxed items, sporting equipment, rarely used jackets, home repair equipment, stored games and sports gear to leave by the trap door.

KEY: A chi enters; B mementos box; C ordered boot rack; D labeled storage boxes; E ski bag; F rack with outdoor jackets; G DIY unit; H storage rack for games and sports items; I chi leaves.

Overloading this area with too much junk can symbolically restrict your higher achievements and aims, and create a fear of what the future may bring.

Empty boxes It always seems a good idea to keep these in case they come in useful for something. However, they waste space and give out stagnant energy. Select several sturdy boxes for emergencies, remove any staples carefully, and fold them flat.

School memorabilia Boxes of old notebooks and awards drag you down. Even if you are proud of your achievements, they are still linking you inexorably with your past.

Boxes of romantic mementos Aging, dusty love letters tied in ribbon along with other special mementos from past relationships tend to give off a musty, sad energy that can be difficult to shift.

Board games and cards Old games and cards, once played every Christmas and holiday, but now hardly used, will create dull, stuck energy.

Old appliances, sports and fitness equipment Cumbersome, rusting equipment takes up space and will probably never be used again. Its bulky presence causes irritation and annoyance.

Family memorabilia Boxes containing reminders of everything that your children ever achieved at school or university again draws you back to the past, restricting new, exciting growth ahead.

Boxes of miscellaneous items A dumping ground for unwanted or discarded items that you never got around to sorting through, this cache of unresolved mess can make you feel stuck and may cause depression.

A refuge for the past

Clearing out the attic is an arduous task, so before you start, assess the extent of the problem (see checklist). If it is dull and musty and so crowded with articles associated with your past life that you cannot move around easily, you have to loosen your grip on the past.

PRESSURE FROM ABOVE

New experiences won't be able to come into your life until you let go of the old ones, symbolized by all the outgrown possessions and mementos stored here. If you have spent most of your life collecting and storing things

and little-used possessions, it may be a sign that you did not relish your life at that time. By tying yourself to the unwanted and unused, you have allowed sentiment to restrict you like a ball and chain. Sloping ceilings will add to the feeling of pressure and being compressed that the attic creates for members of the household.

COLOR, MOOD, AND LIGHTING

The energy in the attic is very yin and passive, and will have a natural tendency to stagnate because normally there are no windows – no outlets – through which energy may escape. Light creams, yellows, or pastel shades of paint will help to make the room brighter and more appealing. Although it is not worth spending a lot on lighting, putting in some spotlights or bulkhead lighting will help to lift the dull energy.

All too often, our past life seems to be stored in the attic (far left) and we hang on to too many sentimental papers (left). Be ruthless and keep only what you really want on efficient shelving units such as these shown (above).

Re-designed space

You may feel exhausted after clearing out the attic, because it contained so many extraneous items from the past, but you now need storage systems for everything that qualifies living there. Plan carefully, as this area can easily become cluttered again, slowing down energy that already struggles to flow freely. Put the items you need to access most frequently near the attic hatch. Create organized space with planned shelving units and durable storage boxes, and you will allow calming energy to float down into the rest of the house.

Basic shelving units are easy to buy and can take care of bulky ski boots or walking shoes. Skis can be stored next to them or in protective ski bags.

ATTIC CLUTTER CHECKLIST

First search through all the junk from your past, sorting it into different piles for the five-bag system (see page 31).

◆ Boxes: these seem so useful but just sit there collecting dust, so throw them out. Keep appliance boxes for the waranty period and then get rid of them.

◆ Schoolbooks, clothes, diplomas, medals, sashes: you know your achievements, so dump these links to your youth.

◆ Love letters, dried flowers, old cards: if you can't bear to part with all of them, keep a few really special items and throw away the rest.

◆ Games and cards: keep the ones that are still used, and give the rest to a hospital or a children's home.

◆ Old equipment such as exercise bikes, baseball bats, and footballs: admit that these will never be used again, and throw out or donate to a school.

◆ Christmas and other holiday decorations: discard damaged items and wrinkled pieces of tinsel.

STORAGE SOLUTIONS

Games and cards Stack favorites neatly on shelving units, putting decks of cards in small cardboard boxes. If there is enough height for freestanding wooden or metal cabinets with wide shelves, these will accommodate a lot of items, otherwise single wooden shelves on metal struts are a budget solution.

Hardwearing boxes on wheels are ideal for the attic as they can be easily moved around.

Love memorabilia Choose a special wicker, rattan, natural fiber, or leather box for these precious mementos, so that it emphasizes the love that you still feel for them. Put it somewhere that is easy to reach, so if you are in a sentimental mood you can get it down to have another look at your treasures.

Ski clothes, other sports clothes, and hiking or walking jackets Put in plastic garment bags to protect them from dirt and dust and hang on clothing rails or store tidily in large, labeled plastic boxes.

Walking or hiking boots Clean well and store on sturdy shoe racks or in large hanging units suspended from a wall hook.

Place your love letters in an appealing box that you will cherish.

Decorations, gardening and home repair equipment, and miscellaneous items Place these in solid plastic or substantial cardboard stacking boxes with lids, and label the contents of each box clearly. Store them in relevant groups, stacked one on top of each other, taking care to make them accessible. Tiny accessories, screws, nails, or other small home repair items can be put into different-sized chest units, with small, labeled drawers, made from plywood or a similar inexpensive wood.

Clutter on the Move

A car can be very much an extension of our personalities – a mobile possession that projects another part of us. So much time is spent in our cars traveling to and from destinations that we form a strong, almost emotional, attachment to it. We choose it partly because of the appeal of its color, style, design, and look. It is our own private little world, where we want to feel safe and secure.

While driving, it is obviously important to stay bright and alert, so the chi in the car needs to be positive and very yang. If your car is a trash can on wheels, the chi will find it difficult to flow around strongly. This can have a profound effect on you, slowing your reactions and decision-making skills, and causing you to drive in a less assured or coordinated way.

THE ENERGY TRAPS

Hoarding things in your car will affect you as much as amassing junk in your home, because you are recreating this disturbed energy on the move. A good clear-out will bring about a major energy shift.

In the trunk This area can become a black hole where piles of articles such as shoes, jackets, or sports equipment are all dumped. This will only become a trunkful of heavy energy, which may disturb your concentration as you are driving around.

ENERGY GRIDLOCK

Chi flows into the junk-filled car and is obstructed by parking tickets, receipts, and discarded CDs. It tries to move over thrown food packaging, toys, and atlases before exiting. In the trunk, chi has problems working around a scrunched-up rug, jackets, sports shoes and car accessories before leaving.

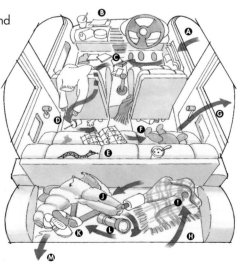

KEY: A chi enters; B parking tickets, receipts and other paper; C piles of CDs; D food and drink cartons; E dumped atlases; F abandoned toys; G chi leaves; H chi enters trunk; I messy rug; J piles of jackets; K training shoes; L car accessories; M chi leaves.

Door pockets and compartments Can you never find the map or atlas you want because there is so much crammed in these storage sections? This sort of clutter can cloud your thinking, making you feel confused.

Seats Are you embarrassed to offer a friend a ride because there is hardly any space for her to sit down? Are CDs, cassette tapes, empty bottles, and parking tickets scattered over seats and floor? Can you never get the seats forward to let people in, because of junk stuffed behind them? This type of disorder may well reflect how you organize your life.

A car is an important possession for most of us, and, like our homes, needs to be regularly assessed for clutter because this slows the chi movement inside it, which can adversely affect our driving skills.

ENERGY FREEWAY

Chi moves into the spruced-up car, proceeds evenly around the CD box and cleared floor into the back over cleaned seats, stored road books, and trash can, and out of the window. Chi comes into the trunk and circulates well around the storage box and car rug before leaving.

KEY: A chi enters; B CD storage box; C cleaned seats; D atlas storage case; E hanging trash can; F chi leaves; G chi enters trunk; H car accessory box; I neatly rolled rug; J chi leaves

A world on the move

Sorting out your car's junk will be a huge relief, but before you get started (see checklist), stand back and look at your car. Do you feel pride when you look at it? Or do you feel ashamed because it is so dirty and shabby? Remember that in feng shui, it is believed that what is going on in our outer life is reflected inside us.

COLOR AND ATMOSPHERE

Color has a strong influence on us, so the color of your car will affect your behavior on the road. In feng shui terms, red is yang and therefore very stimulating; it sometimes causes

Tidy away regularly used items in the door pockets of your car, rather than leaving them on the seats.

anger and irritability, so this may well make you drive faster or aggressively. Yellow is uplifting and encourages an optimistic attitude while driving. Blue and green are calming, as they are more yin (passive) colors, and will create a relaxed atmosphere for driving. Black or gray are very yin; black will give comfort and protection in a car, while gray encourages self-reliance. White and silver are very yang colors – white gives protection, while silver promotes a feeling of harmony and balance when traveling.

Dust and dirt will taint the atmosphere inside a car, so clean it out regularly. Interior surfaces are often plastic and therefore yang. If they are gray, they will shield you from outside influences. Fabric and leather seats are yin, and their softness counteracts the hard yang lines of the plastic. As always, good feng shui requires a balance of yin and yang energies, so there needs to be an equal presence of these two in your car.

Keep all your favorite music for the car in a handy CD box.

STORAGE SOLUTIONS

Road maps and atlases Keep these in the door pockets rather than on or under the seat, or, if you have a lot of them, store them together in a clean plastic briefcase, and place this tidily behind a seat.

CDs, cassette tapes, and books Place these in plastic storage boxes or padded zipped cases which can be stored in the glove compartment or on the back seat.

Litter If you really can't keep this under control, place a small plastic rubbish bin in the car and empty it regularly. Some styles hook on to the car doors.

Miscellaneous car items Put car oil, jumper cables, the tire pump, and other useful car accessories into a sturdy plastic storage box. Make sure it is an adequate size for your needs and comes with a lid so that items don't rattle around loose in the trunk.

CAR CLUTTER CHECKLIST

If your car is a mess, get some bin liners to remove the junk.

◆ Road maps, atlases: search through these carefully, discard out-of-date versions, and give away maps that are no longer needed.

◆ Food wrappers, cartons, empty bottles, parking tickets: search out and destroy all this stagnant energy.

◆ CDs, cassette tapes, and story tapes: keep a select few of your favorites, change these regularly to create new energy, and take the rest back into the house.

◆ Shoes, coats, sports gear, miscellaneous items: these are generating stale energy, so remove them and store indoors.

The Walking Clutter Mountain

If clutter has invaded your home and car, it is likely that this disorganization has spread to the possessions that you carry around with you.

PURSES

These are very personal items, chosen with care. They show an aspect of our personalities, and are linked to the overall style that we like to present to friends and colleagues. So why do so many of us fill them up with useless articles?

If you are trying to portray a positive, confident, organized attitude, owning a bulging, over-loaded purse reveals that there are areas of disorder in your life.

Rather than keeping new phone numbers on scraps of paper transfer them to your Filofax or personal organizer.

Contents overload

Scribbled notes and phone numbers, old shopping lists, vouchers, receipts, restaurant bills, numerous pens that don't work, several hairbrushes, and old make-up – all slow you down by creating pools of dull energy.

Solutions Sort through your bag, throwing away useless papers and pens, and transfer phone numbers to your address book or Filofax. Dispense with old make-up, keep current items in a neat make-up bag, and retain one hairbrush. Remove receipts and vouchers and file in a plastic folder with sections – review this regularly and discard them when no longer needed.

COINPURSES AND WALLETS

Overcrowding these with extraneous matter can have a negative effect on your current finances.

Contents overload Old business cards and out-of-date credit cards, membership cards, appointment cards, and credit card vouchers can all drain your finances.

Solutions Take out the business cards and record useful numbers and addresses in your address book, write appointments in your appointment book, and cut up expired credit and membership cards. File credit card vouchers in a folder and review monthly to keep in order.

BRIEFCASES

Like purses, briefcases reflect some of your character, and contribute to the impression you give to colleagues and clients. Even if you are dressed stylishly, a crammed, shabby briefcase will indicate disorganization and lack of control.

Contents overload Old files, memos, unread reports, unanswered correspondence, broken pens and pencils, reference books – all slow you down and bring in chaos.

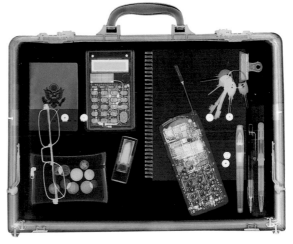

An ordered briefcase will help you stay in control of your working life (above).
Keep paper to the minimum by transferring addresses and appointments to relevant books (left)

Solutions Note the contents of memos and throw them away. Remove files that you don't need and put them back in the office. Create an office action folder for correspondence. Read reports and return them to the office. Throw out old stationery and keep a couple of working pens and pencils in a pocket in your briefcase. Return reference books to their sources. Resolve from now on to carry only the paperwork that you need for meetings or working at home.

Energize with Feng Shui Cures

It's taken time, but you've finally come to terms with your clutter and worked through the emotional loss of throwing away belongings that you have become attached to over the years. You've done a space-clearing ceremony to release any trapped negative energies clinging to your home, but what next? Perhaps the atmosphere around you still feels a bit dull and in need of a lift. For a thorough feng shui analysis, you need the services of a consultant, who can harmonize the home's energies and the surrounding environment. But there are some simple feng shui enhancements and cures that you can apply yourself to raise your home's energy vibrations and make it a brighter, more appealing place to live.

HOW DO THEY WORK?

Enhancements boost the energy around the eight life aspiration areas of the Pa Kua (see pages 14, 15) such as your relationship or wealth corner. Cures can be carefully positioned to offset any problems or correct negative energy affecting the room's

Candlelight is always inspiring and brings in positive yang energy to a room.

atmosphere. For example, healthy plants are positive and yang, and can be used to shield people against harmful cutting chi emanating from a corner or pillar. Plants can also lessen the effects of electromagnetic stress that comes from a television or other electrical equipment.

By harmonizing the energies in each room, you will feel your home start to come alive again and work positively for you.

WHAT CAN YOU USE?

There are several different types of feng shui cure and enhancement that can be placed around your home:

• Mirrors lift energy and expand spaces, but need to be used with caution in the bedroom.

• The soft, tinkly sound of wind chimes is either used to slow down the flow of chi or encourage its circulation in the home.

• Crystals have a strong vibrational energy and their uses include activating the career area, healing, and attracting more energy into a room.

• Water features or aquariums encourage money to flow into your life when placed in your wealth area.

• Lights or candles bring strong yang energy to stagnant areas, or can raise the energy in your fame sector.

• Plants are versatile feng shui cures. Their healthy, positive energy can help alleviate problem areas.

• Attaching bamboo flutes to overhead ceiling beams helps to reduce their negative impact.

• Metal and electrical items enhance the energy of the west.

• Paired items represent togetherness and romance and can strengthen an existing relationship or entice new partners into your life.

• Mirrors shaped like the Pa Kua, situated only outside the home near the front door, help to deflect any bad energy attacking the home.

MIRRORS

In the past, mirrors were considered so special that only people such as pharaohs, kings, and shamans were allowed to use them. In feng shui, mirrors are powerful tools. A flat mirror expands energy, and will open up a narrow space such as a hall, lightening the area and creating the illusion of more space.

Symbolically, a mirror can also "double" energy. So if it is placed opposite a dining table, for example, it "doubles" the value of the food on the table, and is believed to increase the family's wealth. However, don't be tempted to put a mirror opposite your cluttered desk, because it will double your existing workload.

Mirrors also serve the symbolic purpose of making things "disappear". So if your toilet faces the front door, which according to feng shui is a very bad position, putting a mirror on the toilet door will, in effect, make it disappear. Another function of mirrors is dealing with irregularly shaped rooms, which are believed to be inauspicious as they will have a section of the Pa Kua missing. A "missing corner" can be reinstated by using a mirror. For example, if your home has a missing corner in the career

A mirror is very yang, so in a bathroom can help to lift the slow energy that exists there.

area, placing a mirror facing inward on one wall of the L-shape will symbolically restore it.

It is possible to buy eight-sided mirrors shaped like the Pa Kua. These are very powerful, so use them carefully. Never place a Pa Kua mirror inside the home, but it can be hung outside your front door to fend off bad energies such as the cutting chi coming from a road directly opposite. But position it with care, making sure that it does not reflect neighboring homes and send bad energy to them.

Mirror lore

• Never position mirrors facing each other, because they will bounce chi back and forth.

• Don't use a cracked or tarnished mirror, as it literally and symbolically distorts your image.

• Keep mirrors sparkling clean. When not in use, store them face down, otherwise they can bring confusion into your life.

• Do not hang a mirror to reflect your bed, because its energy can cause restlessness and insomnia.

• Never place a mirror opposite your front door, because it will send the good energy that enters out again.

A metal wind chime can lift the chi in the west of a room.

WIND CHIMES

In ancient China, wind chimes were traditionally hung to frighten away unsettled spirits. But nowadays, in modern feng shui, they have a more positive influence in the home. When a wind chime is positioned inside a front door that opens opposite a staircase, for example, incoming chi that would otherwise rush straight up the stairs is filtered and slowed down by the beautiful tinkling chimes. Hung inside or outside, wind chimes ward off negative forces, activate chi, and raise chi in a dull area.

Suspended outside the front door, a melodious five-rod metal wind chime can deflect cutting chi coming off the corners of other buildings.

When choosing a wind chime to lift energy in a room, first find out the room's direction and element so that you know whether to hang metal, ceramic, or wooden wind chimes. In the west (Metal), northwest (Metal) and north (Water is produced by Metal), metal wind chimes are best. Ceramic chimes will suit the southwest (Earth) and northeast (Earth). Wooden chimes work well in the east (Wood), southeast (Wood) and south (the Fire element is produced by Wood).

CRYSTALS

A small, sparkling, lead-faceted crystal sphere dangling in a sunny window spreads an inspiring rainbow of beautiful colors across the walls. Everyone will notice its uplifting effect as it raises the energy vibrations of the room. If you position it in a specific area of the Pa Kua (see page 14), it will bring extra energy to that sector. In your wealth area, for example, you will notice that your bank balance stays healthy and that money seems to come your way more easily.

Crystals are good for energizing areas of your home. Natural quartz (see opposite) can boost your relationship corner in the southwest of your living room.

Hang or place a crystal in a room, after clutter has been cleared out, to create a significant shift in energy flow. Crystals also reduce negativity, deflecting cutting chi aimed at the house by telegraph poles or bus stops. A 1-in crystal sphere is the right size for activating a small room, whereas a $1^{1}/_{2}$-in crystal is better for an average room. Hang the crystal near the top of the window in the center of a pane.

If you are seeking a new relationship, or if an existing one needs some help, a powerful natural quartz cluster can energize the southwest (relationship) corner of your living room, while an amethyst crystal will stimulate the northeast (education and knowledge) sector. Rose quartz is associated with romance, so again place in the southwest. Its soothing qualities will also calm disruptive children, if it is placed in their bedroom.

Crystal tips

• Cleanse new crystals briefly under cold water. If they were bought at a big crystal store, soak them for 24 hours to remove other energies.

• Clean hanging crystals weekly by dipping in still spring mineral water and leaving to dry.

• To activate the powers of a crystal, mentally state your intention for it when you hang it up.

• Amethyst is a wonderful healing stone. Use it to aid recovery from illness.

WATER FEATURES

The trickling sound of flowing water is soothing. Water is a wonderful carrier of good chi into the home. It is also traditionally associated with wealth by the Chinese.

The best place for an indoor water feature is the southeast (Wood and wealth) corner of your home or living room. This is because, in the cycle of the five elements, Water produces Wood.

Choose a small indoor fountain, a trickling water feature or an aquarium. It is preferable to have an odd number of fish in your aquarium, with nine fish considered to be very lucky. Ideally, one should be a different color to absorb negative energy, so eight orange goldfish and one black one would be a good combination. The constant motion of the oxygenated water and the fish stimulate the chi in the water

A pond or small fountain on the left side of your front garden encourages good chi to flow into your home. Fountains also deflect any cutting chi that is adversely affecting your home. Keep water clean and fresh to avoid stagnancy.

Do not put a water feature or image of water in your bedroom, because Water overwhelms Earth in the element cycle (and the bedroom is considered to be Earth). A surfeit of Water is thought to cause relationship problems.

LIGHTING

Lights can bathe a room in soft, warm light, provide localized light for reading, or dramatically light a dinner table. They affect our moods, stimulating or relaxing us. Contemporary lighting is an integral part of interior design and also plays an important part in feng shui. Linking with the Fire element, lights bring positive yang energy to every room. They encourage the flow of chi, particularly in the south. Carefully planned lighting creates balance and harmony.

Where possible, choose table and floor lamps that relate to the element of the areas where they are being placed. For example, rounded, oval, or dome shapes work best in the west and northwest, which link to Metal. Tall, straight lights are appropriate for the east and southeast sections that relate to Wood. Flowing, wavy, or irregular shapes are associated with Water and will enhance areas in the north.

Soft candlelight can promote a relaxing ambience in a room.

CANDLES

Soft, flickering candles bring a natural light and yang energy, and add a special atmosphere to a living or dining room. In the bedroom, candles give off a soft light creating a gentle aura of romance.

Bathrooms are steamy and humid, so energy is very slow-moving here. Candles placed by the bathtub or in wall sconces will lift this energy while imbuing the area with a warm, ambient glow – ideal for a room where we need complete relaxation.

PLANTS

Healthy green plants are living feng shui enhancements that give out oxygen, generating a special chi that engenders a fresher, lively atmosphere. As energizers, they lift stagnant energy in dark corners, and when they are sited near electrical equipment, they help to counterbalance the effects of negative electromagnetic fields. They have the ability to remove toxins from the air, can obscure cutting chi from sharp-angled furniture or columns, and can slow down chi that moves too fast down long corridor.

However, the shape of a plant's leaves is important. Spiky-leaved plants are believed to send out bad chi from their sharp leaves, so choose varieties that have rounded, succulent leaves to attract auspicious chi.

Burning candles in the bedroom brings a romantic feel to this tranquil room.

In the bathroom, plants absorb humidity and raise chi levels, while in a kitchen they can increase the existing yang energy. However, do not place them near an oven or stove top, because their Wood element will fuel the Fire energy of the stove too much.

To enhance and strengthen the Wood element in your home, site plants in the east (associated with family and health) and the southeast (linked to wealth and prosperity). A money plant in your wealth area is believed to mirror your fortunes according to how well it grows. Plants can also help to boost corners in the south of the home (representing Fire, fame and recognition), because Wood feeds Fire in the element cycle.

Index

A
alcoves 36, 51, 58, 72
aquariums 87, 91
arguments 18, 20
aromatherapy 18, 24, 35
attic 29, 74-79
  clutter checklist 78
  color, mood, and lighting 77
  energy traps 74-75
  re-designed space 78
  storage solutions 79
aura, cleansing 22, 24

B
back door 29
bamboo flutes 87
basement 29
bath and beauty products 61, 63, 64
bathroom 28, 30, 60-65, 88, 92, 93
  clutter checklist 63
  color, mood, and lighting 62-63
  energy traps 60, 61
  oasis of calm 62
  storage solutions 64-65
bathroom cabinets and vanity units 61,
  62, 63, 65
baths and sinks 61
bedrooms 8, 32-43, 87, 91, 92
  children's bedrooms 38-43, 90
  clutter checklist 36, 40
  color, mood, and lighting 35, 41
  energy traps 32, 33, 38-39
  storage solutions 36-37, 42-43
beds 34
  bed linen 34, 36, 37
  bunk beds 41
  under-bed storage 33, 35, 39, 43
bills 51, 53
books 36, 37, 40, 42, 55, 57, 58,
  71, 73

boxes, empty 75
briefcases 17, 85

C
candles 35, 57, 59, 63, 87, 92, 93
car 17, 80-83
  clutter checklist 83
  color and atmosphere 82-83
  energy traps 80-81
  storage solutions 83
career prospects 14, 15, 31, 61, 87,
  88-89
chi (energy) 6
  boosting 7, 18, 86-93
  cutting chi 46-47, 48, 57, 69, 87,
    89, 90, 91, 92
  flow 6, 10, 29, 33, 39, 45, 50,
    55, 67, 75, 81, 87, 92
  manipulating and balancing 6, 10
  negative energies 18, 21, 22, 23,
    24, 26, 45, 51, 91
  residual (predecessor) energy 18,
    24
  stagnant energy 8, 16, 18, 25, 39,
    45, 51, 55, 60, 67, 92
children 15
  bedrooms 38-43, 90
Christmas decorations 78, 79
clapping 18, 21, 25
closets 34, 37, 38-39, 43
clothes and shoes 17, 31, 33, 34,
  36-37, 39, 40, 43, 51, 53
clutter hotspots 28-29
coat racks 51, 53
color 35, 41, 47, 52, 57, 62-63, 69,
  77, 82
computers 17, 34, 40, 41, 42-3, 67,
  69, 71
corridors and passageways 29, 92
cosmetics clutter 17, 33, 36, 37, 64

counter tops 45, 49
crystals 69, 87, 90

D
de-junking 32-85
  see also individual rooms and areas
decision-making 15, 66
declutter plan 30-31
desks 28, 51, 66-67, 70, 71

E
education and knowledge 15, 90
electrical appliances 17, 45, 49
electromagnetic stress 41, 59, 69, 87,
  92
emotional attachment to possessions 6,
  8, 12, 16
emotional negativity 20
energy see chi
entrance and hall 10, 17, 28, 29, 50-53
  clutter checklist 51
  color, mood, and lighting 52
  energy traps 50, 51
  layout problems 52
  storage solutions 53

F
feng shui 6, 82, 83
  bad feng shui 57, 63
  colors 35, 82
  cures and enhancements 7, 86-93
  diagnosis 14, 86
  see also Pa Kua
files and filing cabinets 67, 68, 71,
  72-73
floor areas 35, 45, 61, 67
food
  hoarding 46
  storage 45, 48
  friends and contacts 15

G
garbage bags 31
garbage cans 45, 47, 49, 69
glasses and bottles 55, 58, 59
goals, setting 8

H
health 6, 93
herbs 18, 20, 21, 22, 23, 24
home altar 26-27
home repair paraphernalia 51, 53, 79
home study 70
household cleaning products 48, 49,
    64-65

I
illness and death 18, 21, 90
incense burning 18, 21, 26, 27, 57
inherited possessions 6, 13
inner self 8
irregularly shaped rooms 88

J
jewelry 36, 37
junk
    assessing 31
    bagging 31
    hoarding: questionnaire 17
junk mail 8, 11, 51, 53

K
keys 11, 17, 53
kitchen 7, 28, 44-49, 93
    clutter checklist 49
    color, mood, and lighting 47
    energy traps 44-45
    nurturing atmosphere 46-47
    storage solutions 48-49
kitchen cabinets 45
kitchen utensils and gadgets 48

L
liberation 8
life aspirations 14, 15, 86
lighting 35, 41, 47, 52, 57, 63, 69,

77, 92
living room 28, 54-59, 90, 92
    clutter checklist 58
    color, mood, and lighting 57
    comfort zone 56-57
    energy traps 54, 55
    furniture, positioning 56-57
    storage solutions 58-59
love letters 75, 78, 79

M
medicines and first-aid kits 61, 63, 64
mementos and memorabilia 13, 29,
    75, 76, 78, 79
mental clarity 21, 66
mirrors 52, 63, 70, 87, 88-89
misting 18, 20, 21, 24, 26

N
new home 21
newspapers and magazines 17, 36,
    37, 51, 55, 58, 59

O
office 54, 66-73
    clutter checklist 71
    color, mood, and lighting 69
    desk, positioning 70
    energy traps 66-67
open-plan office 70
    siting 70
    storage solutions 72-73
    working environment 68-69
overhead beams 46, 57, 87

P
Pa Kua 14, 15, 31, 69, 70, 86, 87,
    89, 90
paired items 87
photographs 58-59
plants and flowers 63, 65, 69, 87,
    92-93
possessions, outgrown 76, 77
possessions, pruning 13
purses and wallets 17, 84-85

R
refrigerators and freezers 45, 46, 49
relationships 14, 15, 18, 33, 34, 87,
    90, 91

S
salt 18, 21, 26
smudging 18, 20, 21, 22-23
space-clearing rituals 18, 22-27
sports equipment 17, 51, 53, 75,
    78, 79
stairs 51, 52
stationery supplies 73
storage solutions
    attic 79
    bathroom 64-65
    bedroom 36-37
    car 83
    children's bedroom 42-43
    entrance and hall 53
    kitchen 48-49
    living room 58-59
    office 72-73

T
televisions 34, 41, 59
towels and bath mats 63, 64, 65
toys, games, and cards 39, 40, 42,
    75, 78, 79

V
videos, records, CDs, and cassette
    tapes 42-43, 58, 59

W
water features 87, 90-91
wealth and prosperity 6, 14, 61, 66,
    87, 88, 90, 93
wind chimes 52, 87, 89

Y
yang 18, 34, 47, 57, 59, 66, 69, 80,
    82, 83, 87, 92
yin 33, 60, 65, 77, 82, 83

Acknowledgements

I would like to thank Cindy Richards for giving me the opportunity to write this book, and Liz Dean for all her hard work in putting it together. Also Roger Daniels for his great design, and Sam Wilson for her witty illustrations and Kate Simunek for her patience in doing some difficult artworks. My appreciation also goes to my feng shui master Harrison Kyng for setting me off on the wonderful path of feng shui. Finally, thanks to my family and all my friends for their encouragement during the difficult stages of writing, and my boyfriend Steve for his constant support and invaluable advice on clutter in the car.

FURTHER READING

Clear Your Clutter with Feng Shui, Karen Kingston, Piatkus
Creating Sacred Space with Feng Shui, Karen Kingston, Piatkus
Sacred Space, Denise Linn, Rider Books
Clear Your Desk! Declan Treacy, Arrow Business Books
Ligten Up! Free Yourself from Clutter, Michelle Passoff, Harper Perennial
Home Design From the Inside Out, Robin Lennon with Karen Plunkett-Powell, Penguin Arkana
Clutter's Last Stand, Don Aslett, Writer's Digest Books
Feng Shui for Modern Living, Stephen Skinner and Mary Lambert, Cima Books

PICTURE CREDITS

The publishers are grateful to the following for permission to reproduce photographs:
Abode UK: pages 39 above and below, 41,43; Tim Beddow/Interior Archive: page 44; Simon Brown: page 36, 37 centre left; Simon Brown/Interior Archive: pages 19, 40 above, 42 right; Josie Clyde/Stock Shot: page 78; The Cotswold Company: pages 37 above, 42 left, 58, 59 centre, 62, 69, 70, 79 below; Crabtree & Evelyn: page 20; Michael Crockett/Elizabeth Whiting Associates: page 16; Michael Dunne/Elizabeth Whiting Associates: page 51; Laurence Dutton/The General Trading Company: page 53; Feng Shui for Modern Living/Centennial Publishing: pages 30, 31, 52, 86, 89; Filofax: page 85 below left; GettyOne Stone: pages 15, 25, 83 above right; David Giles/Elizabeth Whiting Associates: page 88; The Holding Company: pages 9, 37 below right, 40 below, 59 left, 68, 72 left and right, 83; Jacqui Hurst: page 23 above and below; Rodney Hyett/Elizabeth Whiting Associates: pages 57 and 76; Tom Leighton/Elizabeth Whiting Associates: page 49; Nadia Mackenzie/Interior Archive: page 46; Muji: pages 71, 73, 77, 79 above; Neo Vision/Photonica: pages 11, 21, 66, 87; Michael Nicholson/Elizabeth Whiting Associates: page 91; Osprey by Graeme Ellisdon: page 84; Peugeot: page 82; Pictor International: page 81; The Pier: pages 32, 35, 59 right, 63, 92, 93; T. Sawada/Photonica: page 90; Fritz von der Schulenburg/ Interior Archive: pages 34, 54, 65; Karin Taylor/ Marie Claire/IPC Syndication: page 27; Pia Tryde/The General Trading Company: page 13 above; The White Company: page 64 above and below; Elizabeth Whiting Associates; page 48; Henry Wilson/Interior Archive: page 13 below, 56, 60.